The Virginia DUI Handbook:

Answers to 14 Common Questions and Everything Else You Need to Know about DUIs.

2nd Edition

Luke J. Nichols, Esq.

For questions and comments, contact:

Luke J. Nichols at
The law firm of Nichols & Green pllc
Fairfax, Va 22030
(703) 383-9222 (ph)
(703) 383-9220 (fx)
lnichols@nicholsgreen.com
www.nicholsgreen.com

ISBN: 978-0-9828928-4-8
Spectrum Publishing
Fairfax, Va

Table of Contents

Introduction   1

Chapter 1: "Is That Illegal?"   3
A Description of the Laws Related to DUI in Virginia

Chapter 2: "How Bad Is It?"   16
The Costs and Consequences of Conviction

Chapter 3: "What Should I Do if I Am Arrested?"   36
How to Avoid Being Arrested for DUI in Virginia, and What to Do
if You Are Arrested

Chapter 4: "Can They Really Do That?"   57
Your Rights Before and During Arrest

Chapter 5: "Did I Really Fail the Test?"   66
A Quick Guide to Field Sobriety Tests, PBTs, and Breathalyzers

Chapter 6: "Do I Have a Chance?"   88
Why Drivers Should Never Assume They Will Be Found Guilty

Chapter 7: "Do I Really Need an Attorney?"   105
The Top Ten Reasons to Hire an Attorney

Chapter 8: "How do I Hire an Attorney?"   113
A Guide to Attorney-Client Contracts and the Retention Process

Chapter 9: "How Do I Find a Good DUI Attorney?"   117
How to Spot a Bad Attorney and What to Look for in a Good One

Chapter 10: "How Do I Get Out of Here?"   123
Being Arrested, Making Bail, and Getting Your Car out of Impound

Chapter 11: "What Do I Need to Do to Prepare for Trial?"   128
How to Get the Most out of Your Attorney

Chapter 12: "Can I Drive Yet?"   134
What Happens to Your License after Arrest and Conviction

Chapter 13: "What Is Going to Happen at Trial?"   148
What to Expect on the Day of Trial

Chapter 14: "Should I Appeal?"   159
The Pros and Cons of Appealing a Conviction

Introduction

The saddest part of my job is sitting in court day after day, watching people go to jail and lose their licenses because they did not understand the judicial system and did not understand their rights. This book will not only help you find better attorneys but also empower you to use your attorney more effectively by becoming a more informed client. Virginia's DUI laws are complicated and brutal: if you have been arrested, you need to read this book.

In Virginia, the crime of driving under the influence (DUI) is one of the most complicated crimes in the Commonwealth. There are roughly 22 pages of criminal code and approximately 17 different punishments associated with DUIs. Defending a DUI may require knowing dozens of highly technical forensic processes, understanding constitutional issues, and navigating mountains of bureaucratic red tape.

DUIs are also extremely serious. A driver's first DUI can mean up to 12 months in jail and a mandatory 12-month revocation of your driver's license. It can also cost a driver up to $2,500 in fines, in addition to fees, court costs, and increased insurance premiums. Second and third DUIs are more complicated and much more serious.

Anyone arrested for DUI or refusal to submit to a breath test needs to hire an experienced DUI attorney. This book will not only walk you through the entire DUI judicial process, it will also teach you how to work effectively with your attorney.

The best DUI attorneys have invested substantial time and resources studying DUI forensic and legal issues. They are detail-oriented, are easy to communicate with, have excellent negotiating and people skills, back up their promises with a free appeal, and (most importantly) will represent their client through the entire DUI judicial process.

Good attorneys will aid their clients in getting a restricted license. They will also help their clients register for the extremely tedious and complicated mandatory drug and alcohol programs.

Without this post-trial help, clients may be arrested for unintentionally violating their probation or their restricted license. Make sure you hire an attorney who will assist you through the post-trial process.

If you have been arrested for DUI or refusal to submit, I hope that you will take the time to read this book carefully. Educated clients not only hire better attorneys, they get more out of the attorneys they hire.

Chapter 1:
"Is That Illegal?"
A Description of the Laws Related to DUI in Virginia

If you are reading this book, you probably have a lot of questions about what the law in Virginia says you can and cannot do. To know the law, you must first know which level of government you are dealing with, and who is enforcing the laws.

There are several levels of government: city/town, county, state and federal. Each has its own laws regarding drinking and driving, and each may have its own police force.

State troopers enforce state law. The county police and sheriff's department enforce state and county laws. The municipal police enforce municipal ordinances, but they can also charge people under state codes. Other law enforcement officers, such as university police, usually only enforce state laws.

In the Commonwealth of Virginia there are 95 counties and 39 independent cities (such as Alexandria, Fairfax City, and Hampton). Inside those counties are towns which may have their own semi-independent judicial system (such as Vienna, Spotsylvania, and Herndon).

Each county, independent city or town has the ability to create laws in addition to those created by the level of government above them. Consequently, if you are arrested for DUI, you can be charged with violating the state law, the county code, or perhaps even a town or city ordinance.

The laws on federal land are a little different. Drivers arrested in national parks fall under the jurisdiction of the National Park Service, and they are tried in federal courts and punished under federal law (i.e. the Code of Federal Regulations). However, civilian drivers arrested on military bases in Virginia or on federal facilities such as the Pentagon are tried under the laws of the Commonwealth of Virginia, even though the trials take place in federal courts.

State, county, and city DUI laws are usually the same but sometimes there can be major differences. It is always very important to present your summons or arrest warrant to your attorney so he or she can know exactly which law you are being charged with violating and in which jurisdiction you are required to appear.

Despite the many differences in state, county, city, and federal laws, the vast majority of Virginia drivers are charged under the state laws of Virginia or under local laws that are essentially the same as the state laws. Consequently, for the sake of space, this book will only cover Virginia's state laws.

DUI (Driving Under the Influence)
DUIs are one of the most complicated criminal laws in Virginia, and having a competent attorney to represent you is absolutely essential. There are approximately 22

pages of DUI codes, endless case law on the subject, and 17 different categories of punishments that a driver can receive depending on how many convictions he has, his blood alcohol content (BAC), whether a minor was in the car, and the discretion of the judge.

However, there are only five ways to be convicted of a simple DUI. Va. Code § 18.2-266 lists all five:

1) Operating a motor vehicle while having a blood alcohol content (BAC) of .08 or above;

2) Operating a motor vehicle while under the influence of alcohol or substantially impaired;

3) Operating a motor vehicle while under the influence of any drug that impairs your ability to drive safely;

4) Operating a motor vehicle while under the influence of any combination of drugs and alcohol which impairs your ability to drive safely; and

5) Operating a motor vehicle while having more than very small and specific amounts of cocaine, methamphetamines, PCP, or ecstasy in the driver's blood.

The most common way someone is convicted of DUI is by having a blood alcohol content (BAC) of .08 or higher. The law does not require a driver to be drunk to commit a DUI. An experienced drinker may be convicted of DUI no matter how safely he operates his vehicle if his blood alcohol level is over .08.

The same is true for cocaine, meth, PCP, and ecstasy. Even if the driver was not dangerously affected by the drugs at the time he was driving, he can be convicted of DUI if his blood contains more than a specified amount of one of those drugs.

Drivers can also be convicted of DUI when they have a BAC of less than .08 but are "substantially impaired". Substantial impairment means that the driver's ability to drive was impaired by alcohol.

Erratic driving behavior is the most common evidence of substantial impairment. Consequently, a driver who is texting or talking on a cell phone with a BAC of .07 may be arrested for DUI and have their distracted driving used as evidence of intoxication.

DUI is not just for alcohol. Any drug that affects your ability to drive safely can potentially lead to a DUI conviction. Over-the-counter allergy medicines, cough syrup, necessary prescription medications, and seemingly innocent drugs can affect your ability to drive and result in a DUI conviction.

In Virginia, any medication or drug that affects your ability to drive can theoretically result in a DUI.

"Operating" Defined
Frequently, police arrest intoxicated drivers who are sitting behind the wheel of a parked car. The question is whether sitting in a parked car is "operating" a vehicle.

In Virginia, a vehicle is in operation if the defendant is behind the wheel and the keys are in the ignition and certain electrical or mechanical systems are engaged. This may be true even if the vehicle is immobilized (e.g. is stuck in a ditch or has a flat tire).

If you are charged with DUI but the officer did not see you behind the wheel or if the officer did not see the engine on, contact an attorney immediately to discuss whether the commonwealth can prove you were "operating" the vehicle.

Public Roads versus Private Roads
Some of the DUI and refusal laws only apply on "public highways" in Virginia. However, do not be fooled. "Public highway" really means any road surface "open to the public" including most toll roads.

If a person is caught driving on private property, such as a parking lot or driveway, then the issue is whether that road surface is "open to the public". The presence of towing signs, "No Trespassing" signs, a gate, etc., are all factors that may determine whether a road surface is open to the public.

This issue is a very technical legal issue, and should be brought to your attorney's attention immediately.

Involuntary Intoxication

What happens if you were not voluntarily drunk or intoxicated? Involuntary intoxication is an affirmative defense to DUI. When someone did not intentionally ingest drugs or alcohol or was not aware of the nature of what he was ingesting, he may not have committed a DUI.

The most common example of involuntary intoxication is when someone takes a new prescription medication that has an unusual and unforeseen side effect while driving.

DUI for Drivers Under 21 (Baby-DUI)

Do not let the name fool you. Baby-DUI is every bit as serious as a standard DUI. Va. Code § 18.2-266.1 makes it illegal for anyone under 21 to drive while he has a BAC of .02 or higher. Many underage drinkers do not realize that they can be arrested for DUI after having very little alcohol.

If a person is under 21 and has a BAC of .08 or more, they can be charged with the normal DUI or Baby-DUI.

DUI After Driver's License is Revoked, Suspended, or Restricted

According to Va. Code § 18.2-272 (B), it is a crime for certain persons who have had their license revoked, suspended or restricted, to drive with a BAC of .02 or more. This law is problematic for drivers with restricted licenses, who think they can have two beers and sti drive because they are not drunk.

The consequences of a conviction of 18.2-272 are very similar to DUI, but a conviction means no restricted driver's license for one year and can also result in the driver's car being impounded for up to 120 days.

Refusal to Submit to Breath or Blood Testing
Va. Code § 18.2-268.3 states that every person who is arrested for DUI within three hours of driving on any public highway in Virginia has to submit to a breathalyzer test, a blood test, or both.

However, before charging a driver with refusing to take a test the police officer who arrested the driver must first read a form explaining the refusal law to the driver. Then that officer must offer the driver one more chance to comply with the test. If the officer does not fulfill both of these requirements, the refusal charge and the DUI may be dismissed. Talk to an attorney immediately if you were not informed of the consequences of refusal or if you were not given another chance to take the test.

Transporting a Minor While Under the Influence
Va. Code § 18.2-270(D) increases the penalties for a DUI if the crime was committed while there was a minor (anyone under 18) in the car. These penalties include mandatory jail time and increased fines.

If you are arrested for DUI with a minor passenger in the car, make sure you inform your attorney as soon as possible.

DUI Related Child Abuse/Neglect
Being arrested for DUI while having a minor in the car can, in more egregious cases, can be considered felony child abuse under Va. Code § 18.2-371.1(B). The Virginia Court of Appeals has upheld cases where mothers arrested for DUI were also convicted of felony child abuse because the court believed that driving drunk with a minor in the car demonstrated "reckless disregard" for the life of the child.

DUI and Maiming
In addition to the various codes dealing with vehicular homicide, Va. Code § 18.2-51.4 creates a special felony for anyone who severely injures another person while driving under the influence. Conviction can result in up to five years in prison, indefinite loss of license, lawsuits, and many other extremely serious consequences.

Drinking While Driving (Open Containers)
Under Va. Code § 18.2-323.1, it is a crime to drive on any public road while drinking alcohol. Possessing an open container of alcohol in the passenger compartment is sufficient evidence for the prosecution to prove drinking while driving. Driving while drinking or driving with an open container can affect the outcome of a DUI case so talk to your attorney if you had any alcohol or containers in the car.

DUI While Driving a Commercial Vehicle

Drivers of commercial vehicles can be charged under the normal DUI statute or under special DUI laws that are unique to commercial vehicles.

Va. Code § 46.2-341.24(A) is exactly the same type of crime as a normal DUI with its five different ways of being found guilty. However, Va. Code § 46.2-341.24(B) states that a driver can be arrested for DUI if he is driving a commercial vehicle with a BAC of .04 or more.

Drivers who have a commercial driver's license (CDL) should not hesitate to get an attorney if they are arrested for DUI or similar offenses. The consequences of DUI are much more serious for drivers who have CDLs.

CDL holders cannot get restricted driver's licenses after a DUI conviction even if their DUI was not committed in a commercial vehicle.

Wet Reckless

Va. Code § 46.2-852 defines "reckless driving" as driving in a manner so as to endanger the life, limb or property of any person. "Wet reckless" simply means the driver is charged with reckless driving instead of DUI.

Reckless driving is still a serious criminal charge, but police officers sometimes charge drivers with reckless driving when they don't have sufficient evidence of DUI. Typically, this happens at the scenes of accidents or when the driver has a low BAC.

Drunken in Public (DIP)

Va. Code § 18.2-388 makes it a crime to be intoxicated while in public. This charge may be used in cases where the officer cannot prove that the defendant was driving the vehicle.

Assault/Battery on an Officer

Assault under Va. Code §18.2-57 is a grossly misunderstood charge that is often used as leverage against a driver who has been aggressive with officers during a DUI arrest. "Assault and battery" means any harmful or offensive touching, or putting someone in immediate fear of harmful or offensive touching. A touch does not have to hurt or injure to be battery, and it does not even have to make contact to be assault.

Poking an officer in the chest, waving your fingers in his face, taking a swing, kicking, or even thrashing around could potentially be an assault on a police officer even if no one was hurt.

Assault on a police officer in Virginia is a Class 6 felony and carries up to five years in prison (with 6 months of mandatory jail time) and a $2,500 fine.

If you were charged with assault on an officer or even if the officer threatened to charge you with assault, tell your attorney immediately. It may be used against you in your DUI trial.

Obstruction of Justice

A person being investigated for DUI can be charged with obstruction under Va. Code §18.2-460 when he 1) obstructs law enforcement officers in the performance of their duties, 2) threatens or attempts to intimidate officers, or 3) knowingly makes false statements to police officers who are investigating another driver or person. Refusing to cooperate with law enforcement usually is not enough to prove obstruction of justice.

Obstruction of justice is a Class 1 misdemeanor and is punishable by a maximum of 12 months in jail and a $2,500 fine. If you are accused of (or even threatened with) obstruction, notify your attorney immediately.

Resisting Arrest (Misdemeanor Fleeing)

Under Va. Code §18.2-479.1, "resisting arrest" means fleeing from the police after the police try to arrest you. Fleeing can mean running or walking only a few steps. Falling to the ground, curling up in a ball, or pulling your hands away from police may not be sufficient to prove resisting arrest.

Resisting arrest is a Class 1 misdemeanor and is punishable by a maximum of 12 months in jail and a $2,500 fine. If you are arrested for DUI, just relax and call your attorney. Resisting arrest may be used against you in your DUI trial.

Eluding (Car Chase)

If a driver refuses to pull over their car after police order them to, that driver may be charged with eluding police under Va. Code §46.2-817. Simple eluding is a Class 2 misdemeanor (up to six months in jail). However, if a driver endangers others, then eluding becomes a Class 6 felony (up to five years in prison). Eluding comes with a mandatory license suspension that will last from 30 days to 12 months. This suspension will be in addition to any loss of license because of a DUI.

If the officer who pulled you over claims you were refusing to pull over, notify your attorney immediately even if you were not charged with eluding. Accusations of eluding may be used as evidence of intoxication in your DUI trial.

Bribery of a Police Officer
When people are arrested for DUI they can sometimes say things that they later regret. If a driver offers anything to a police officer in exchange for "letting them go" this may be interpreted as attempting to bribe a police officer, which is a Class 4 felony in Virginia.

Even if you were just "kidding", tell your attorney immediately if you made any such statements to a police officer or if the officer accused you of making such offers. Even if you were not charged with bribery, such behavior may be used against you in your DUI trial.

Driving on a Suspended, Revoked or Invalid License
There are several criminal offenses that involve drivers' licenses. Va. Code § 18.2-272 makes it a crime to drive after a license has been revoked for DUI, refusal or other

related offenses. Conviction comes with up to 12 months in jail, a mandatory one year loss of license with no restricted licenses and up to 120 days of vehicle impound.

Va. Code § 46.2-391(D) is for driving on a suspended license when the license was suspended for multiple DUI convictions. Driving when suspended for multiple DUI convictions always requires mandatory jail time, but if the driving behavior is dangerous or if the driver was intoxicated, then Va. Code § 46.2-391(D) becomes a felony with one year of mandatory jail time and a maximum of five years in prison.

Va. Code § 18.2-301, driving on a suspended license, is the most common license crime. It requires a person to drive after they were banned or suspended from driving. However, to convict a driver of driving on a suspended license, the officer must prove that the driver had been properly notified about their suspension. Driving on a suspended license can result in jail time, an additional license suspension, and fines.

Driving without a valid license under Va. Code §46.2-300 is also a criminal offense. It comes with jail time, a license suspension, and fines.

Chapter 2:
"How Bad Is It?"
The Costs and Consequences of Conviction

About the time the police put the handcuffs on, the driver realizes that he or she is in trouble. The first thing they want to know is "How bad is it?" DUIs are very serious in the Commonwealth of Virginia. They come with complex and severe punishments.

Because DUIs evoke so much public attention and because of the problems with repeat offenders, almost every year the legislature makes the consequences of a DUI more complicated and more serious. If a driver hires an attorney who does not focus their practice on DUI defense, that driver runs a greater risk that his attorney will arrive at court unaware of recent changes in the law. Additionally, because DUI laws change so frequently, drivers should not attempt to use this book as a substitute for consulting with an experienced attorney.

DUI laws are complicated; there are 17 different types of punishments, programs, or fees that result from a DUI conviction. The punishments that a person could receive depend on how many prior DUI convictions he has, his blood alcohol content (BAC), whether there was a minor in the car, and the discretion of the judge.

Some punishments are mandatory and others are discretionary. Some consequences are decided by the judge; others are decided by the Alcohol Safety Action

Program ("ASAP") case managers, the DMV, or other third parties.

Because these consequences are so severe, complex, and far-reaching, it is essential that you have an attorney that will take the time to get to know you and your situation so that they can counsel you on how your legal decisions will affect your life. A good DUI attorney must know their client as well as the law.

As mentioned above, the different punishments for DUI depend on many things, including: the number of convictions a driver has had, the time that has elapsed since those convictions, his BAC at the time of arrest, whether there were aggravating factors (such as having a minor in the car), and the judge.

The number of convictions a driver has is an important factor in determining how much trouble a driver is in. A driver's second conviction in ten years carries mandatory jail time, and his third DUI in ten years is a felony.

Prior convictions from most jurisdictions in Virginia and even from some states and federal jurisdictions can be used against you if the prosecution can comply with a series of strict evidentiary rules. An experienced DUI attorney will know these requirements and may be able to thwart the prosecution's efforts to use prior convictions against you if they do not comply with the evidentiary rules.

If you have ever been convicted of or arrested for DUI (even if it was in another state, as a juvenile, or long ago), you need to hire the best attorney you can afford and explain your legal history thoroughly.

Make sure your attorney has a copy of your DMV record and tell your attorney: 1) the exact dates of your prior arrests and convictions; 2) which jurisdiction your prior convictions were in 3) the outcome of your cases and 4) whether you were represented by an attorney for each conviction.

The effects of prior convictions for DUI are influenced by how much time has passed since your last DUI. A second or third DUI in five years is more serious than a second or third DUI in ten years. Once again, if you have been previously arrested for DUI, you need to hire a quality DUI attorney immediately.

Jail Time

When people come into my office, they are usually most concerned with how much jail time they will get. To answer that question, you need to know that there are two types of jail time: discretionary jail time and mandatory jail time.

Discretionary jail time is the amount of jail time that the judge can choose to give a defendant. Discretionary jail time for misdemeanors is also usually served twice as fast if the defendant behaves himself in jail. For every two days of discretionary jail time you receive, the sheriff's department will usually only make you serve one day. So if a driver is given a discretionary sentence of 30 days, then he will usually only spend 15 days in jail (conditional on good behavior).

On the other hand, if the law requires mandatory jail time, those days in jail cannot be waived by the prosecution, judge, or sheriff. Therefore, a driver who is found guilty of a crime that carries mandatory time in jail must serve 100% of that mandatory time.

Occasionally sheriffs and judges will allow defendants to participate in jail programs such as "work release" or "weekday release" while they are serving mandatory jail time. The same rule applies to alcohol/drug inpatient rehabilitation, house arrest, or electronic monitoring. Talk to your attorney about local rules and the likelihood of these options.

A driver convicted of a first DUI faces up to 12 months of discretionary jail time. However, if that driver's Blood Alcohol Content or "BAC" was .15 or more, he will receive five days of mandatory jail time. If his BAC was more than .20, then he will receive 10 days of mandatory jail time.

A second DUI conviction carries 12 months of possible jail time. Of those 12 months, ten to 40 days will be mandatory jail time, depending on the BAC and whether the last conviction was within the last five or ten years.

A third DUI conviction is a felony and comes with up to five years in prison. 90 or 180 of those days are mandatory depending on whether the three prior convictions were within ten or five years respectively. A fourth DUI has one year of mandatory jail time and four years of discretionary incarceration.

Not all jail sentences are equal. An attorney may ask the judge to allow the defendant to turn himself in at a later date. Jail time can sometimes be served on weekends, and drivers who may be incarcerated for substantial periods of time can apply for work release programs, inmate trustee programs, house arrest, or electronic monitoring—to name just a few programs.

The availability and details surrounding these programs vary widely between counties and cities, and may even vary based on which day of the week the driver is convicted (for example, Alexandria's week-end jail program is hardest to get into on Fridays, but is easier to get into on Mondays).

It is essential to have an attorney who knows the local programs and can guide you through the application process.

License Suspension
Next to going to jail, the worst thing that can happen to most people is losing their driver's license. Unfortunately, Virginia is extraordinarily strict about taking away peoples' right to drive. There are three types of license suspensions that can affect a person charged with DUI in Virginia:

1) An Administrative Suspension
The police confiscate your license on the day you are arrested.

2) A Judicial Suspension
The judge suspends your license, and the bailiff confiscates your license upon conviction.

3) A DMV Suspension
The DMV sends you a letter stating that you no longer have the right to drive because of excessive demerit points or for administrative reasons.

Administrative Suspension
Administrative suspension, found in Va. Code § 46.2-391.2, occurs when the arresting officer notifies the driver that his license has been suspended. This notification usually happens at the police station after the officer administers a breath test. If you have a Virginia driver's license, the arresting officer will confiscate it.

The police can suspend an out-of-state license holder's right to drive in Virginia, but they are not allowed to confiscate an out-of-state license and cannot revoke an out-of-state driver's right to drive in other states. If the police confiscate your out-of-state driver's license, notify your attorney immediately for help getting your license back from the police.

Administrative suspensions apply to drivers who are charged with refusal to submit to a breath or blood test *or* DUI based on a BAC of .08 or more (.02 or more if they are under 21). There should be no administrative suspension for an adult DUI arrest without a BAC of .08 or more. If the police suspend your license for DUI without a BAC of .08 or more, then contact your attorney immediately to get the suspension removed.

Administrative suspensions last only seven days for first time offenders, but drivers with prior convictions will be suspended for 60 day or until the day of trial, depending on whether they were arrested for their second or third DUI. Drivers can appeal an administrative suspension and/or receive a restricted driver's license during the suspension period.

An effective DUI attorney may be able to get you your license back or get you a restricted license during the administrative suspension. Consequently, the sooner you hire your attorney, the more services you can get for your money. Retain an attorney immediately after your arrest to maximize the benefits you can receive from your attorney.

Judicial Suspension
The second way that Virginia may revoke your right to drive is through the judicial process. If a person is found guilty of his first DUI, the judge *must* suspend his license for 12 months. A second offense requires a mandatory suspension of three years. A third or fourth offense will result in an indefinite suspension of the right to drive.

A driver's first conviction for refusal to submit to a breath/blood test results in a 12-month license suspension (without a restricted license) in addition to any suspension period received for DUI. A second conviction for refusal will result in a three-year suspension without a restricted license.

If convicted, you must give up your Virginia driver's license on the day you are sentenced so prepare alternative forms of ID (such as a passport). The court issued restricted driver's license is not a valid form of photo ID. 30-60 days after receiving the court issued restricted license the driver must take their temporary court-issued restricted license to the Virginia DMV to get the official restricted license which is also a photo ID.

The judicial suspension period begins when the judge issues his sentence, whether or not a driver turns over their license. But the first day of the twelve month or three year suspension period does not start until the driver turns over their Virginia license to the bailiff or court clerk. The longer you wait to turn over your Virginia license the longer your suspension period will be.

The Virginia judicial system cannot revoke, confiscate or suspend an out-of-state driver's license. But the court will revoke the driver's right to drive in Virginia and will do so for the same period of time as for a Virginia driver. The out-of-state driver may lose their license if their home state chooses to revoke their license due to their Virginia DUI or refusal conviction.

After a DUI conviction the court may grant a restricted driver's license. However, CDL holders and most out-of-state drivers will not be granted a restricted license in a Virginia court.

Restricted driver's licenses are by definition restrictive. A restricted driver's license limits the times and places you can drive. These restrictions must be strictly obeyed or the driver may be charged with driving on a revoked license.

A first-time offender may be granted a restricted license immediately upon conviction, but a second DUI conviction in ten years means no restricted license will be granted for four months. If the second DUI conviction is within five years, the driver must wait one year to apply for a restricted license. A three-time offender must wait three years to apply for a restricted license.

All drivers convicted of DUI must have ignition interlock installed on all of their cars in order to be granted a restricted license. The drive must also pay for the interlock system's monthly maintenance, its installation, and additional court costs.

After six months the driver may petition the court to remove the ignition interlock if they have had no failing tests during that time.

A driver cannot get their license reinstated without installing ignition interlock on at least one car for at least six months. Ignition interlock is mandatory even if the driver choses to go without a restricted driver's license or does not own a car.

DMV Suspension
Even if the court grants a driver a restricted license, the DMV may yet take that privilege away for accumulating excessive demerit points or for administrative reasons.

Any Virginia driver who commits a moving violation (including DUI) will have up to six points deducted from his driving record. These points are called demerit points. Accumulating too many demerit points in too short a period of time can result in the suspension of the driver's license.

Almost all of the DUI and DUI related offenses (including refusal) are six-point offenses. The DMV has complete control over the point system, and your judge cannot alter the point assessed against you once you are convicted.

For drivers who are minors, any demerit point conviction means they must attend a driver-improvement class. Failure to do so within 90 days results in a license suspension until the program is completed. A second point conviction results in a 90-day license suspension. A third will result in a suspension of one year or until the offender reaches age 18, whichever is longer.

For adults, the accumulation of eight demerit points in 12 months or 12 points in 24 months results in an advisory letter from the DMV.

The accumulation of 12 demerit points within 12 months or 18 points in 24 months results in a mandatory driver-improvement class followed by six months of probation and 18 months of control period. The driver-improvement program must be completed within 90 days or the license will be suspended until the course is completed.

The accumulation of 18 points in 12 months or 24 points in 24 months results in a mandatory 90-day license suspension. Once that period has expired the driver must complete a driver-improvement class before their license can be restored. After restoration, they will be on probation for six months and then a control period for 18 months.

If the driver is convicted of a traffic offense while on DMV probation, his license will be suspended. The driver's license will be suspended for 45 days for a three-point violation, 60 days for a four-point violation, and 90 days for a six-point violation. Once that individual finishes the suspension period, he will be placed on probation for an additional six months and then 18 months on the control period.

A violation while on the control period will result in the driver being placed on probation for six more months followed by another 18 months of control period.

Consequences of Demerit Points in Virginia (Adult Drivers)		
	within 12 months	within 24 months
8 points	Letter from DMV	Nothing
12 points	Mandatory driver-improvement class + probation for six months	Letter from DMV
18 points	Mandatory 90-day license suspension + driver-improvement class + probation for six months	Mandatory driver-improvement class + probation for six months
24 points	Mandatory 90-day license suspension + driver-improvement class + probation for six months	Mandatory 90-day license suspension + driver-improvement class + probation for six months

A driver who is suspended for their first probation violation may request a restricted license from the DMV. DMV issued restricted licenses are similar to court issued restricted licenses but the application process is completely different. If you are arrested for DUI while on DMV probation, make sure you hire an attorney who is familiar with the DMV restricted license application process.

Drivers should *always* get a copy of their driving record before trial so that they can determine whether they are in danger of a DMV suspension. DMV suspensions are dangerous in DUI cases because they can cause a driver to lose their court issued restricted license.

The DMV can also administratively revoke or suspend a Virginia driver's license. This situation can occur if a Virginia driver receives a DUI in another state. An administrative suspension can also occur if the DMV believes a driver is not physically or mentally able to operate a vehicle safely. This type of suspension happens most often with elderly drivers.

And an administrative suspension will also occur if a judge fails to impose a mandatory license suspension. For example: if a Virginia driver is found guilty of refusal to submit to a breath test and the court does not suspend the driver's license for a full year, or if the court grants a restricted license, the DMV will revoke that license for 12 months.

Effects of a DUI on Insurance
After a conviction for DUI, a driver's insurance premium can increase dramatically depending on the insurance carrier, previous driving history, and other factors. For a second DUI conviction, the premiums can go up even higher. These rates will remain high for three years or more, for your first offense. A single DUI can increase

insurance premiums more than all of the other fines and fees combined.

Some insurance carriers will refuse to insure a driver convicted of DUI. The driver may be required to get SR-22 (high-risk driver) insurance and then file proof of SR-22 insurance with the DMV before the DMV will reinstate the driver's license.

Fines

Excluding insurance hikes, a driver's first DUI can cost $1,000 to $4,200 in fines, government fees, and costs. A second DUI costs $1,200-$5,500. A third or fourth DUI costs $2,100-$5,800.

There are approximately 14 different fines, fees, and costs that may be assessed against a defendant if he is found guilty. Here is a list of some of those expenses and their approximate dollar amounts:

- fines ($250-$2,500),
- license reinstatement fee ($175),
- ignition interlock system ($70 plus $60/month),
- ignition interlock court cost ($20)
- ASAP ($495+),
- the Trauma Center Fund ($50),
- court costs ($100),
- jury fees ($210/day),
- court-appointed attorney fee ($120 for misdemeanor, $445 for felony),
- restricted license fee ($220),

- mandatory driver-improvement class ($35-75),
- car impounding fee ($120 plus $50/day).

[*Caution: these amounts are constantly changing and should only be used as estimates*].

If you cannot pay all of your fines and fees immediately talk to your attorney. Many courts offer payment plans, deadline extensions or even except community service in exchange for payment. Before your trial, talk to your attorney and discuss the local payment options in your jurisdiction. Many of these options can affect your ability to get a restricted license, and some require approval from your judge.

Alcohol Safety Action Program (ASAP)

A mandatory condition of probation for anyone convicted of DUI is that the driver must complete the Virginia Alcohol Safety Action Program (VASAP or ASAP). The defendant must register for the ASAP classes within 15 days after sentencing or release from jail. Failure to register for ASAP within 15 days will result in a loss of the restricted license and a probation violation. Also, the Virginia DMV will not restore driving privileges after the suspension is over if the driver did not successfully complete ASAP.

At the driver's first ASAP appointment, the driver will have an intake interview and be assigned a case manager who will decide which classes the driver should take. Most first time DUI defendants who do not have substance abuse issues will be assigned to a 20-hour, 10-

week program that meets once a week at the same time every week for two hours per session. This program is the cheapest at about $495 (*costs change frequently and should be used only as an estimate*).

However, if a driver is convicted of a second DUI, had a high BAC, or if the ASAP program believes the driver has substance abuse issues, the ASAP case manager may require the driver to attend more rigorous and more expensive classes. A driver may be required to attend meetings multiple times a week or even every day. ASAP can require in-patient or out-patient drug or alcohol rehabilitation. ASAP can demand that a driver attend meetings for longer than just ten weeks. These more extensive programs can cost thousands of dollars. The ASAP case manager has massive amounts of control over the form your ASAP treatment may take.

If a driver does not live in Virginia, the ASAP program may allow the driver to attend a similar private or government program in their home state. It may also be possible for a person to substitute the ASAP program with treatment at a private facility. Contact an experienced DUI attorney for help navigating ASAP.

The two most common ways people fail ASAP is by missing too many classes or by using drugs or alcohol while enrolled in ASAP. Violating the terms of ASAP can result in a probation violation and serious jail time. Additionally, Virginia will never restore driving privileges if a driver does not successfully complete ASAP.

Make sure you hire an attorney who can explain and aid you in navigating the ASAP probationary process. Talk openly with your attorney if you doubt your ability to attend all of the classes or abstain from drugs and alcohol.

Probation and Suspended Sentences

Typically, a judge will hand down a sentence with the majority of jail time suspended (For example: "60 days in jail, 50 days suspended"). Suspended jail time is jail time you do not have to serve, conditional on your successful completion of ASAP, and "keeping the peace" for a period of time (usually one year).

This sentence is a form of "inactive probation." Inactive probation means that you are on probation but do not have to report to a traditional probation officer.

If a driver violates the conditions of his probation (does not attend ASAP or gets convicted or any crime) during that year, then the driver will appear before the judge at a "show cause hearing" to determine how much of their suspended sentence they will have to serve. Many judges will sentence violating drivers to the entire suspended sentence.

Talk to your attorney immediately if you are on bond, bail, pre-sentence release, probation, parole, inactive probation, DMV probation, or have any suspended sentences. These conditions can be extremely important to your DUI case even if they are from other states, happened long ago, or are unrelated to DUI.

Other Possible Consequence of DUI or Refusal
There are many possible consequences of a DUI or refusal conviction that are unique to an individual client. These consequences may be loss of job, loss of custody of children (especially if the client is in the middle of a custody dispute), denial of college or graduate school admission, denial of security clearance, denial of application to the armed services, loss of a CDL, immigration issues, and potential civil liability.

To effectively represent you, a DUI attorney needs to know more than just the facts of your case. Your attorney needs to know you personally so that he or she can counsel you on all of the possible consequences. Make sure you hire an attorney who takes the time to get to know you. Also communicate to your attorney how you believe a DUI conviction will affect your life.

Refusal to Submit to a Breath Test
Refusal to submit to a breath test can be either a civil or criminal offense. Refusal to submit with no prior convictions of refusal or DUI is a civil offense (not criminal) and will result in a suspension of driving privileges for one year with no opportunity for a restricted license.

Virginia courts cannot suspend an out-of-state driver's license. They may only ban an out-of-state driver from driving in Virginia. However, an out-of-state driver's home state may choose to administratively suspend their license because of a refusal conviction in Virginia.

Being convicted of refusal to submit within ten years of being convicted of a DUI or a prior refusal will result in a three-year suspension of your driver's license (with no restricted license), up to six months in jail, and up to $1,000 in fines. A driver's second refusal is a criminal offense.

If a person refuses to submit after two convictions of DUI or refusal (or a combination of the two) within the last ten years, he will lose his driving privileges for three years (with no restricted license), face up to 12 months in jail, and a maximum fine of $2,500.

Driving suspensions for DUI and refusal to submit will run back-to-back. That means a person who is convicted of his first DUI and first refusal to submit at the same time will lose his driving privileges for two years and will not receive a restricted license until after the first year. A person who is convicted of a second DUI and a refusal to submit will have his license suspended for six years (three for the second DUI and three for refusal to submit).

# of Offenses	1st	1st	1st	2nd	2nd	2nd
Years	NA	NA	NA	5 yr	5 yr	5 yr
BAC	.08-.149	.15-.20	.20+	.08-.149	.15-.20	.20+
	Misd 1	Misd 1	Misd 1	Misd 1	Misd 1	Misd 1
Max Jail Time	12 mth	12 mth	12 mth	12 mth	12 mth	12 mth
Mandatory Jail	0	5 dy	10 dy	20 dy	30 dy	40 dy
Max Fines	$2,500	$2,500	$2,500	$2,500	$2,500	$2,500
Mandatory Fines	$250	$250	$250	$500	$500	$500
Adminstrative Suspension	7 dy	7 dy	7 dy	60 dy	60 dy	60 dy
License Revoc/Suspension	1 yr	1 yr	1 yr	3 yr	3 yr	3 yr
License Reinstatment Fee	$175	$175	$175	$175	$175	$175
Forfeiture of Car	No	No	No	No	No	No
Ignition Interlock	Mandatory	Mandatory	Mandatory	Mandatory	Mandatory	Mandatory
IIS Fees	$70 + $60/mth	$70 + $60/mth	$70 + $60/mth	$70 + $60/mth	$70 + $60/mth	$70 + $60/mth
Restricted License	0 dy	0 dy	0 dy	1 yr	1 yr	1 yr
Restricted License Fee	$200	$200	$200	$200	$200	$200
ASAP Fee	$495+	$495+	$495+	$495+	$495+	$250-$300
Trauma Center Funds	$0	$0	$0	$50	$50	$50
Court Costs	$100	$100	$100	$100	$100	$100
Min. Cost	$1,020.00	$1,020.00	$1,020.00	$1,270.00	$1,270.00	$1,270.00
Max Cost	$4,260.00	$4,260.00	$4,260.00	$4,980.00	$4,980.00	$4,980.00

# of Offenses	2nd	2nd	2nd	3rd	3rd	4th
Years	10 yr	10 yr	10 yr	5 yr	10 yr	10 yr
BAC	.08-.149	.15-.20	.20+	NA	NA	NA
	Misd 1	Misd 1	Misd 1	Fel 6	Fel 6	Fel 6
Max Jail Time	12 mth	12 mth	12 mth	5 yr	5 yr	5 yr
Mandatory Jail	10 dy	20 dy	30 dy	6 mth	90 dy	1 yr
Max Fines	$2,500	$2,500	$2,500	$2,500	$2,500	$2,500
Mandatory Fines	$500	$500	$500	$1,000	$1,000	$1,000
Adminstrative Suspension	60 dy	60 dy	60 dy	60 dy	60 dy	60 dy
License Revoc/Suspension	3 yr	3 yr	3 yr	Indefinate	Indefinate	Indefinate
License Reinstatment Fee	$175	$175	$175	$175	$175	$175
Forfeiture of Car	No	No	No	Yes	Yes	Yes
Ignition Interlock	Mandatory	Mandatory	Mandatory	Mandatory	Mandatory	Mandatory
IIS Fees	$70 + $60/mth	$70 + $60/mth	$70 + $60/mth	$70 + $60/mth	$70 + $60/mth	$70 + $60/mth
Restricted License	4 mth	4 mth	4 mth	* 3 yr	* 3 yr	?
Restricted License Fee	$200	$200	$200	$200	$200	$200
ASAP Fee	$495+	$495+	$495+	$495+	$495+	$495+
Trauma Center Funds	$50	$50	$50	$50	$50	$50
Court Costs	$100	$100	$100	$450	$450	$450
Min. Cost	$1,270.00	$1,270.00	$1,270.00	$2,120.00	$2,120.00	$2,120.00
Max Cost	$5,460.00	$5,460.00	$5,460.00	$5810.00+	$5810.00+	$5810.00+

Punishments, fines and costs for DUI.

35

Chapter 3:
"What Should I Do if I Am Arrested?"
How to Avoid Being Arrested for DUI in Virginia and
What to Do if You Are Arrested

Each section of this chapter is dedicated to one of the
many things you can do to prevent being pulled over,
arrested, or convicted of DUI. Whether explaining when
to call a taxi or how to prevent being confused for a
drunk driver, this chapter is meant to empower drivers. It
teaches them how to avoid being pulled over, arrested, or
convicted of DUI.

How Much Can You Drink and Still Drive?
There are five ways to be convicted of a simple DUI
under Va. Code § 18.2-266:

1) Driving while having a blood alcohol content (BAC)
of .08 or above;

2) Driving while under the influence of alcohol;

3) Driving while under the influence of any drug that
impairs ability to drive safely;

4) Driving while under the influence of any combination
of drugs and alcohol which impairs ability to drive
safely; and

5) Driving while having more than very small and
specific amounts of cocaine, methamphetamines, PCP, or
ecstasy in the driver's blood.

The law does not require a driver to be drunk to commit a DUI. The most common way people are convicted of DUI is by having a blood alcohol content (BAC) of .08 or higher. While a BAC of .08 usually means a person is demonstrating the physical symptoms of intoxication, an experienced drinker may be able to operate his vehicle normally with a BAC of.08. However, such a driver may still be convicted.

For a driver under 21 years old, the legal limit is only .02. It can take only one or two beers for a minor to reach a BAC of .02. Drivers under the age of 21 should not drive in Virginia after drinking any alcohol.

An adult driver can also be convicted of DUI with a BAC of less than .08 if they are driving impaired. Drivers may be found guilty of DUI if the police officer can prove that alcohol was negatively affecting their driving ability. A driver who is sleepy, texting, or talking on a cell phone after having only a few drinks may be easily mistaken for a driver under the influence of alcohol.

DUI is not just for alcohol. Any drug that affects your ability to drive safely can potentially cause you to be convicted of DUI, especially when the drug is used in combination with alcohol. Over-the-counter allergy medicines, cough syrup, necessary prescription medications, and other seemingly innocent drugs can affect drivers' ability to drive and result in a DUI conviction. Strictly follow the dosage instructions as well as all warning labels for medications, especially if you will be consuming alcohol.

Since you can be convicted of DUI with either an elevated BAC or intoxicated behavior, it is important to know how each drink affects your BAC as well as how it affects your ability to drive.

BAC can be estimated with the Widmark formula, which can be simplified into two charts: one for men and one for women.

These charts predict the BAC at or around one hour after the drinks have been consumed. BAC drops at an average rate of about .015 every hour after the body has absorbed all the alcohol in the stomach (usually one hour after a person stops drinking on an empty stomach).

Therefore, a person who has a BAC of .11 and an empty stomach needs to wait at least three hours before he will be below .08 and almost seven-and-a-half hours before he may be completely sober. If a person ate while drinking, it will take them more time to sober up.

(*Caution: these time and drink estimates are averages and should be used only as rough estimates. Individuals may vary*).

Things like size, body fat content, the speed at which the drinks are consumed, and whether the driver ate while drinking can affect alcohol absorption rates and metabolism rates.

Blood Alcohol Content (BAC) for Men									
One drink with 0.5 fl. oz. alcohol by volume									
	Body Weight (kg/lbs)								
Drinks	40 kg	45 kg	55 kg	64 kg	73 kg	82 kg	91 kg	100 kg	109 kg
	90 lb	100 lb	120 lb	140 lb	160 lb	180 lb	200 lb	220 lb	240 lb
1	–	0.04	0.03	0.03	0.02	0.02	0.02	0.02	0.02
2	–	0.08	0.06	0.05	0.05	0.04	0.04	0.03	0.03
3	–	0.11	0.09	0.08	0.07	0.06	0.06	0.05	0.05
4	–	0.15	0.12	0.11	0.09	0.08	0.08	0.07	0.06
5	–	0.19	0.16	0.13	0.12	0.11	0.09	0.09	0.08
6	–	0.23	0.19	0.16	0.14	0.13	0.11	0.1	0.09
7	–	0.26	0.22	0.19	0.16	0.15	0.13	0.12	0.11
8	–	0.3	0.25	0.21	0.19	0.17	0.15	0.14	0.13
9	–	0.34	0.28	0.24	0.21	0.19	0.17	0.15	0.14
10	–	0.38	0.31	0.27	0.23	0.21	0.19	0.17	0.16

Figure 1: BAC Calculation Chart for Men

Blood Alcohol Content (BAC) for Women									
One drink with 0.5 fl. oz. alcohol by volume									
	Body Weight (kg/lbs)								
Drinks	40 kg	45 kg	55 kg	64 kg	73 kg	82 kg	91 kg	100 kg	109 kg
	90 lb	100 lb	120 lb	140 lb	160 lb	180 lb	200 lb	220 lb	240 lb
1	0.05	0.05	0.04	0.03	0.03	0.03	0.02	0.02	0.02
2	0.1	0.09	0.08	0.07	0.06	0.05	0.05	0.04	0.04
3	0.15	0.14	0.11	0.1	0.09	0.08	0.07	0.06	0.06
4	0.2	0.18	0.15	0.13	0.11	0.1	0.09	0.08	0.08
5	0.25	0.23	0.19	0.16	0.14	0.13	0.11	0.1	0.09
6	0.3	0.27	0.23	0.19	0.17	0.15	0.14	0.12	0.11
7	0.35	0.32	0.27	0.23	0.2	0.18	0.16	0.14	0.13
8	0.4	0.36	0.3	0.26	0.23	0.2	0.18	0.17	0.15
9	0.45	0.41	0.34	0.29	0.26	0.23	0.2	0.19	0.17
10	0.51	0.45	0.38	0.32	0.28	0.25	0.23	0.21	0.19

Figure 2: BAC Calculation Chart for Women

Please remember: a driver can be arrested even though his BAC rate is below .08 if he is intoxicated. Inexperienced drinkers or people who cannot hold their liquor may act drunk more than other people with the same BAC. Other conditions may affect the appearance of intoxication, such as fatigue, medications, or disabilities.

In order to prevent being arrested for a DUI despite a low BAC, it is best to know how alcohol or medication affects you before you try to drive. Always err on the side of caution.

Also, many medications and alcohol do not mix. Small amounts of alcohol and normally mild medicines may have a powerful combined effect. Read the warning labels of any medicine you are taking, and ask your doctor before you decide to drink while on any medication (over-the-counter or prescription).

Medications

You never know exactly how new medications will affect you. Read warning labels carefully and be careful when driving after taking new medications. While the law might forgive someone who has an unusual reaction to medication while driving, you will need a good criminal defense attorney to avoid a conviction in that situation. Also, be extremely careful about drinking alcohol while on any medication.

Sleep Deprivation

Alcohol is a sedative. The effects of sleep deprivation mimic those of intoxication. A sleepy driver may have blood shot eyes, poor coordination, and perhaps even slurred speech. A sleepy driver who has the odor of alcohol on his breath is even more likely to be confused with an intoxicated driver. Always avoid driving when you are tired, but especially avoid drinking even small amounts of alcohol and then driving when you are tired.

Diabetics

Drivers with diabetes who are suffering from imbalances in their blood-sugar/insulin may exhibit signs of intoxication. Extremely low blood sugar can cause symptoms such as slurred speech, poor muscle coordination, dizziness and poor balance.

Diabetic ketoacidosis can also cause the production of acetone in the body of diabetics which can cause some diabetics' breath to smell like they have been drinking wine. If you have diabetes and are ever accused of DUI you should make your condition very clear to the officer and ask for medical attention immediately. A blood-sugar test could help prove your innocence.

Low-Carb Dieters

Driver's on aggressive low-carb diets can exhibit symptoms of intoxication including the odor of alcohol on their breath. As the body becomes deprived of carbohydrates it produces ketones which eventually convert into isopropyl alcohol. The isopropyl alcohol is disposed of in the bodies breath, urine, etc.

This causes a low-carb dieter to smell like they have been drinking. If the same driver is fatigued, has poor balance, or below average muscle control, an officer may mistake them for an intoxicated driver. Low-carb dieters should be extra careful to avoid the appearance of intoxication or situations that could draw attention from law enforcement.

Sobriety Checkpoints

In Virginia, the police periodically set up sobriety checkpoints to inspect random drivers for intoxication. There are a number of laws and procedures in Virginia that regulate how sobriety checkpoints work.

The police department usually announces checkpoints on the "news" section of its website. These locations are announced so that drivers can avoid the traffic problems caused by these checkpoints.

Another important rule about sobriety checkpoints is that the police must use an objective method for choosing which cars to stop prior to beginning the checkpoint. Profiling is not allowed.

However, suspicious or illegal behavior may cause a person to be pulled over despite not being chosen for the investigation.

The most common example is when a driver makes an illegal U-turn to avoid a checkpoint. The police can pull that driver over for an illegal U-turn. If the driver had executed a legal maneuver and was not driving suspiciously the police would not be able to stop him.

The final rule about sobriety checkpoints is that checkpoints must minimize the time that each driver is stopped. The officer cannot make you step out of your car unless there is some evidence of illegal or suspicious activity. For DUIs, these signs include the smell of alcoholic beverage on the breath, slurred speech, blood shot eyes, confusion, poor motor skills, among others.

If the officer decides that the driver displays signs of impairment, he will be asked to pull over to a separate area where the officer will continue the investigation.

Right to Remain Silent and Field Sobriety Tests
In determining whether a driver is intoxicated, police officers use a variety of clues, tests, and machines. However, the most effective tools they use are their mouths. Officers do not ask casual questions, they gather evidence.

Police will ask several kinds of questions. "Have you have had anything to drink?" "How much have you had to drink?" "When did you have your last drink?" "Where did you drink?" If nothing else, they want you to talk to them so that they can tell whether you are slurring your speech, are incoherent, or have alcohol on your breath. Do not answer any questions.

During a traffic stop, an officer may or may not have the right to order you to do any number of things including asking you to step out of your car or searching you and your car. However, even if an officer does not have the legal right to do something, he or she can always ask and get permission.

Legally, there is a fine line between an officer ordering you and an officer asking you to do something. If you ever have any doubts about whether you are required to obey police officers, clearly and politely ask them whether they are *ordering* you.

If they are not ordering you to do something, you can decline. If they are ordering you, politely obey the order and hire a good attorney. Any evidence found by violating a driver's rights may not be admissible in court.

Police officers look for erratic driving, empty or open alcoholic beverage containers, glassy or blood shot eyes, slurred speech, and confusion. When they see any combination of these things, they may decide to ask you to perform a field sobriety test (FST).

FSTs are a series of completely voluntary exercises or tests used to determine sobriety prior to arrest. Many of these tests are difficult and can easily be failed by a sober person. You are not required by law to submit to any FST. The police cannot make you take them. Never take any FST.

If an officer orders you to take an FST, the results of that FST may be excluded from evidence at your trial. If you feel that the officer in your case pressured or manipulated you into taking an FST notify your attorney immediately.

The FSTs used by the police in Virginia vary between regions, jurisdictions, and individual officers. Often, officers use variations of the same test that may or may not be more complicated. Most of the tests examine two things: 1) muscle control and 2) ability to follow instructions.

Do not take an FST. FSTs are meant to be difficult, and some sober people cannot pass them. Because these tests measure the ability to follow instructions, the tests begin as soon as the officer is speaking. Failure to follow any instruction is considered evidence of intoxication.

Some of the typical tests include:

- walking heel-to-toe on a straight line, and then turning and walking back a specific number of steps;
- standing on one leg without moving your arms or legs;
- saying the alphabet, starting from a random letter and progressing forward;
- counting between two given numbers, either forward or backward;
- touching your nose
- touching your thumb and fingers in a specific order;
- performing the Rhomberg Balance test (close eyes, tilt head back, and stand still for 30 seconds); and
- the Horizontal Gaze Nystagmus (HGN) test.

Of course, performing the physical aspects of these tests gracefully is important, but the driver must also follow the instructions exactly. Often, the police officer is talking quickly over the noise of traffic, and the driver is trying to pay attention while under large amounts of stress.

Wind, rain, snow, temperature, lighting, headlights, gravel, uneven pavement, lightning, thunder, passengers, language barriers or even the police officer can distract the driver and cause him to fail.

Do not be bullied into taking a field sobriety test. They are 100% voluntary and drivers never do as well as they think they will. If you have a physical or mental condition that prevent you from performing well on these tests, do not take the any of the tests and tell your attorney immediately.

One of the least understood field sobriety test is the Horizontal Gaze Nystagmus (HGN) test. Nystagmus is when a person's eyes quiver involuntarily. Everyone's eyes exhibits at least a minimal amount of nystagmus under natural conditions but this shaking can become exaggerated under certain conditions, including intoxication.

Police officers will perform this test by asking the driver to follow a finger or a pen with his eyes as they move it slowly back and forth in front of the driver's face. They will often shine their flashlight in your eyes while doing this in order to observe any eye tremors.

The HGN test is actually several tests. The officer first looks for a lack of "smoothness" as the eyes track back and forth. The officer then looks for tremors when the eye is looking to the extreme left and right, and then the officer looks for tremors while the eye is looking at an angle that is less than 45 degrees from center. And sometimes the officer looks for tremors while the driver looks straight upwards. The driver will be utterly unaware of whether or not their eye is shaking, and the shaking is uncontrollable.

HGN can be caused by preexisting medical conditions or onsite conditions. Few people are aware if they have preexisting or induced nystagmus, therefore they cannot inform the police that they have a condition that invalidates the test. Drivers should not submit to the HGN test.

There is rarely anything to be gained by taking any FST. FSTs are voluntary; you do not have to take them and refusing to take an FST is very weak evidence of guilt.

Tell the Officer if You Are Overheated
Few people know how breathalyzers work, and fewer realize how common it is for breathalyzers to produce faulty readings.

Breathalyzers are machines that estimate a person's Blood Alcohol Content (BAC) by measuring the amount of alcohol fumes in a person's breath. Alcohol enters into the lung as it evaporates from the blood. Breathalyzers estimate BAC by assuming that the concentration of alcohol fumes in the lungs is constantly proportional to the amount of alcohol in the blood. However, as with all assumptions, there are flaws.

Anyone who has taken a hot shower knows that the warmer a liquid becomes, the more it evaporates (or steams). Blood alcohol is the same. As a person's temperature increases, alcohol escapes from the blood into the lung at higher concentrations.

Because breathalyzers do not take a person's breath temperature; the breathalyzers simply assume that the person's breath temperature is average (34° Celsius). However, if the driver's breath temperature is above average, the concentration of alcohol fumes in the lungs will be excessively high and the machine will return an erroneously high BAC reading. Consequently, if a person has a fever, is dressed too warmly, or is even left in a hot police car too long, his breath test results may be erroneously high.

If you are arrested for DUI and are hotter than normal, let the arresting officer know. Roll down the window, sit by the fan, drink water, and make sure that the arresting officer knows you are too hot.

Tell the Police about Any Medical Conditions
Drivers who submit to a breath test should notify the arresting officer of their medical conditions, especially if they have diabetes, are on a low-carb diet, have a gastro-intestinal disorder or decreased lung function. These conditions may cause erroneously high BAC readings.

Some examples of medical conditions that can cause erroneously high BAC readings are: acid reflux, Gastroesophageal Reflux Disease (GERD), gastric bypass surgery, Irritable Bowel Syndrome (IBS), chronic or extreme heart burn, Chronic Obstructive Pulmonary Disease (COPD), bronchitis, or asthma. If a driver who has been arrested for DUI has any of these, or similar conditions, they should notify their attorney immediately.

Vomit, Burping, and Mouth Alcohol
Another flaw with breathalyzers is that officers assume that all the alcohol detected came from the driver's lungs. Alcohol fumes from a person's stomach, mouth, or throat may be much more potent than the fumes from the lungs. A person that has recently consumed alcohol, burped, or vomited may produce a BAC breath result that is much higher.

Because of this problem, police officers in Virginia must "observe" the driver for 20 minutes before administering a breath test at the police station. Officers are supposed to look for signs that the driver has burped or vomited in order to validate the results.

If you regurgitated, hiccupped, vomited, or burped 20 minutes before taking a breath test, make sure you let the officers know so that they can reset the clock and allow another 20 minutes for the alcohol fumes to evaporate.

Be careful, people who intentionally make themselves vomit or burp to avoid being tested might be charged with refusal to submit to a breath test.

Do Not Blow With Anything in Your Mouth
Breathalyzer machines are designed to measure the small concentrations of alcohol vapors in human lungs. The

relatively strong fumes produced by having alcohol residue in your mouth will result in higher readings.

If a driver has any foreign objects (food, dentures, gum, piercings, braces, retainers, etc.), trace amounts of alcohol may be hidden in or around those objects. If any of the residual alcohol or fumes gets blown into the machine then the BAC results will be increased. Foreign objects can also damage the machine and interfere with a driver's ability to blow properly.

Never take a breathalyzer test with a foreign object in your mouth. If you had anything in your mouth less than 20 minutes prior to taking a breathalyzer test then notify your attorney.

Know When You Can Refuse to Blow and When You Cannot

There are two types of breathalyzers used in Virginia: 1) the Preliminary Breath Tester (PBT) and 2) the Evidential Test Device (ETD). The biggest difference between these machines is that the PBT is voluntary. You have the right to refuse a PBT. However, you may be charged with refusing to blow into an ETD.

PBTs are handheld devices that police officers use at the scene of the arrest to determine BAC prior to arrest. They are usually kept in the trunk of a police cruiser. They are small, portable machines with a plastic tube or mouthpiece that the driver blows into. PBTs can only be used to justify an arrest; they cannot be used as evidence of intoxication at trial.

ETDs are different from PBTs in several ways. They are not portable. The machine is about the size of a large shoebox with a blow tube that sticks out from the side.

ETDs are also usually attached to a printer and keyboard. All ETDs in Virginia are the same make and model (the INTOX EC/IR II's), and they are found at the police station rather than kept in police cars.

An ETD: the INTOX EC/IR II

A PBT: the Alco-Sensor III

Before blowing into an ETD in Virginia, a driver must be observed for 20 minutes. If the driver refuses to blow into an ETD, he must be read a form letter stating that he is required to submit to the test. The driver must also be told that he has the right to observe the ETD results, and that he has a right to receive a copy of the printed results. The results of an ETD *can* be used as evidence at trial.

Remember, the most important difference between PBTs and ETDs is that a driver suspected of DUI does not have to blow into a PBT, but a driver arrested for DUI *must* submit to being breath-tested by an ETD. Always refuse a PBT.

Pay Attention to Possible ETD Operator Errors
Drivers who are arrested for DUI and brought to the police station to be tested with an ETD breathalyzer must be observed for at least 20 minutes before they can be tested. If at any time the driver burps, vomits, or places anything in his mouth, the driver's mouth must be cleared out, and he must be observed for another 20 minutes.

Because a driver may not always inform an ETD operator when they have burped or vomited, it is up to the operator to constantly observe the driver prior to and during testing. The operator should not be performing other tests, leaving the room, or doing anything that distracts them from watching the driver for the entire 20 minutes prior to testing. If your operator let someone else perform the observation, or if they were distracted during the 20 minute period tell your attorney.

Before testing, the officer administering the ETD test must inform the driver that he has the right to observe the results of the test on the digital screen (not just on the print out). Every driver tested in Virginia should exercise his right to observe the results for themselves. The driver should tell his attorney immediately if the officer does not inform them of these rights.

When a driver is ready to take the ETD breath test, he will blow at least two times. The machine will take two samples and then print out the lesser of the two readings. If the machine detects any errors, an error screen will appear, and the machine will print out an error message that may be used as evidence of refusal to submit to a breath test. If the machine has severe problems it may shut off completely.

If you had to blow more than twice, if any error messages appeared or if the machine ever turned off, make sure you inform your attorney. If the operators had trouble performing your test or the tests of other drivers while you were waiting, inform your attorney of that as well.

Blowing Into a Breathalyzer 101
There are many urban myths about how to fool breathalyzers, and most of them are false. When people try to fool the machine, they usually end up getting charged with refusal to submit to a breath test and DUI. The machines are built to detect some of these tricks, and the officers have seen many of them before.

If you decide that you are going to submit to a breath test there are a few things you should know. A driver who holds his breath before blowing into a breathalyzer may artificially increase the BAC reading by 5%, while a driver who hyperventilates may decrease his BAC result by more than 10 %. That is a 15% difference. Do not take a large gulp of air before blowing as it will only increase your results.

Most officers and breath technicians believe that there are more alcohol fumes in the deep recesses of a person's lungs than there is at the top of the lungs. Consequently, the police want you to take a great big breath and blow really hard, so that you exhale as much of that alcohol-rich air in the bottom of your lungs as possible. Do not fall for it.

Most breathalyzers require 1500 cubic centimeters of breath. That's about two to three seconds of uninterrupted breath. But they do not require the person to blow hard.

Blowing extremely hard, puffing, stopping, or sucking in sharply at the end will cause a false reading. Often, a driver will be instructed to blow extremely hard and when they do it causes the machine to register "invalid test". If a driver produces too many "invalid test" results the operator may believe that the driver is playing games with the machine and charge them with refusal to submit.

Blow as you would normally blow through a straw, not as if you are trying to blow up a balloon. If you have any conditions that stop you from blowing steadily at normal pressure (such as asthma, bronchitis, chest congestion, etc.), notify the officer before taking the test and notify your attorney afterwards.

If you decide to submit to the ETD test remember these steps.

- Do Not blow hard, like you are blowing up a balloon.
- Do Not take a big deep breath or hold your breath before blowing.
- Do Not stop and start while blowing.
- Do Not try to pretend to blow.
- Do Not try to suck your breath out of the machine.

But Do:

- Pay attention for possible operator errors
- Blow slow and steadily for about three seconds.
- Breathe normally before blowing.
- Notify the police officers if you have any medical conditions that affect your lungs.
- Notify the police if you burp or regurgitate at any point before or during the test
- Tell the police if you have any foreign objects in your mouth including dentures or braces.
- Always ask to see the digital readout of your results and keep the printed copy of the results.

How to be Respectful to Officers While Standing Your Ground

Being respectful to police officers is always a good idea. Most officers are good people doing a good job. It can also be a benefit to you if you have treated the police with respect.

The police have control over whether your car gets impounded, parked, or picked up by friends. Also, the police tend to be much less likely to charge nice people with refusal to submit to a breath test, obstruction of justice, or other related charges.

Perhaps the biggest advantage to being nice to police officers is that, in almost every jurisdiction, the prosecution talks to the officers and asks for their opinion before offering to make a deal or drop the charges. Often, the first question the prosecution asks the officer is, "What were they like?"

However, it is important to stand up for your rights. When you talk to the police, be straightforward and clear with phrases such as: "I am not going to answer any questions", "I am not going to take any field sobriety test or submit to a PBT" or "I would like to please see the results of my breath test." As stated above, if you ever have any doubts about whether you are required to obey police officers, clearly and politely ask them whether they are *ordering* you.

If they are not ordering you to do something, don't argue, just say "No." If they are ordering you, politely and silently obey the order and hire a good attorney. Any evidence found by violating a driver's rights is not admissible in court, so do not lose your temper if an officer violates your rights.

Chapter 4:
"Can They Really Do That?"
Your Rights Before and During an Arrest

In order to enjoy your rights, you have to exercise them. Even if police officers cannot force you to do something they can always ask. There is almost nothing an officer cannot do if you give them permission. Unfortunately, it is not always easy to tell when an officer is asking and when an officer is demanding; both tend to be equally intimidating.

Legally, there is a fine line between when police officers are ordering you to do something and when they are asking you to do something. If an officer says, "Please get out of the car," is that officer asking you or ordering you to get out? If the officer is asking and you step out of the car, then you may have consented to give up the right not to be removed from your car.

If you ever have any doubts about whether you are required to obey a police officer, clearly and politely ask them whether they are *ordering* you. If they are not ordering you to do something, refuse. If they are ordering you, obey the order and hire a good attorney. Any evidence found by violating a driver's rights may not be admissible in court.

What Is My Right to Remain Silent?
In a DUI stop, you do not have to answer any questions. You only have to show your driver's license and your

registration. If you must obey a direct order from a police officer, do it in silence.

Remember that police officers' most effective tools are their mouths. Officers never ask casual questions. When a police officer approaches you, everything the officer says is calculated to extract evidence. Officers are good at what they do.

In a DUI situation, police will ask you several questions: "Do you know why I pulled you over tonight?" "Have you had anything to drink?" "How much have you had to drink?" "What did you have to drink?" "When did you have your last drink?" "Where were you drinking?"

These questions are designed to collect evidence against you. If nothing else, they want you to talk to them in order to see whether you are slurring your speech or have alcohol on your breath.

Officers may use any part of your conversation as evidence against you. Comments which seem innocent to you may be harmful at trial. For example: If you do not answer questions quickly the officer may testify that you were slow and unresponsive (presumably because you were drunk). If you say that you are lost or if you don't know exactly which street you are on then it may be interpreted that you were so drunk you did not know where you were.

Do not talk to the police, whether you are in your car, on the side of the road, in the police cruiser, at the jail, or in front of a magistrate. Everything can be used against you. Simply hand them your ID and registration, and say nothing. Then hire the best attorney you can afford.

What Is My Right to an Attorney?
Your right to an attorney means that you have the right to have an attorney present during an interrogation. It also means that you cannot be tried and sentenced to jail without the opportunity to have an attorney represent you in court.

The right to have an attorney at trial can affect drivers who are accused of having prior DUI convictions. If a driver is on trial for a second, third or fourth DUI the prosecution must prove that the defendant's prior convictions were constitutionally valid.

This means that the prosecution must prove that the defendant either had an attorney or waived their right to an attorney at their prior DUI trials. If you are on trial for a subsequence DUI and you did not have an attorney at your previous DUI trial, notify your attorney immediately.

The constitutional right to an attorney does not give drivers a right to have an attorney present for a breathalyzer test. Officers will not allow you to call or consult an attorney before taking a breathalyzer test.

The right to have an attorney present during an interrogation becomes an issue most frequently in either serious DUI cases (such as after a fatal accident), hit-and-run cases, or when serious felony charges are associated with the DUI. Most people accused of DUI are not interrogated and are released on bond before they have an opportunity to call an attorney.

However, once you are released, contact an attorney immediately. Several key defenses and rights you have may expire if you wait too long to hire counsel. Also, an attorney may be able to get your license back sooner or aid you in getting your vehicle out of impound.

What Are the Miranda Rights?
On television, when the bad guy is arrested, the police say something along these lines: "You have the right to remain silent. Anything you say or do may be used against you in a court of law. You have the right to an attorney. . . ."

These rights are called the *Miranda* rights, and the police are not allowed to interrogate someone who has been placed in custody until they have told that person their *Miranda* rights. If the police interrogate you after arrest but before being read your *Miranda* rights the results of that interrogation may be inadmissible in court. The best way to protect your Miranda rights is to remain silent throughout the entire DUI stop, arrest, and booking process.

Do I Have to Take Field Sobriety Test (FST)?
FSTs are a series of exercises or tests used to determine sobriety prior to arrest. Many of these tests are difficult and can easily be failed by a sober person. Any test that

you take on the side of the road is completely voluntary (including the Preliminary Breath Test "PBT"). The police cannot make you take any field sobriety tests. Never submit to field sobriety tests.

Can They Impound My Car?
When a driver is arrested, if their car is not already legally parked, the car gets towed and impounded. The impound yard charges the owner about $120 plus $60 per day. However, if the police are in a good mood (and there is a sober, licensed driver nearby), the police might let the other driver take the car home or park it. The police will not park your car for you. One of the advantages of being polite to the police is that they will be more likely to let someone park your car or drive it home for you.

If your car is legally parked or if there is a sober driver present who can take the car home and the police impound the car anyways, it may be because they want to search the car. If the police legitimately impound a vehicle they are allowed to do a limited search of the vehicle and they can use what they find in the car against you in court.

If the police impounded your car even though it was legally parked or even though there was a person to drive it away, tell your attorney because your rights may have been violated by the police in order to search your car.

Can They Search My Car? Can They Search Me?
The police can search anyone, anywhere and anytime—*if* they are given legitimate permission. Consequently,

police usually ask to search whether they have the right to search you or not. If you willingly allow them to search, it does not matter whether the search was justified. Never agree to be searched!

Some drivers agree to a search because they believe they are being pressured to consent. If the police use intimidation tactics, if they phrase their request like an order, if they make any threats, or if they repeatedly ask for permission, your consent may not have been valid. Evidence that is discovered through these tactics may not be admissible in court.

If the police used intimidation to get your consent to search, or if you felt you did not have a choice, tell your attorney immediately. Any evidence found through aggressive tactics may be excluded from court even if you allowed the police to search.

If the police search without consent, then the police must have probable cause or one of the many exceptions to the probable cause requirement. If the police searched you or your property without consent then talk to your attorney about whether that search may have been unconstitutional.

Do You Have to Use a PBT Breathalyzer?
In the Commonwealth of Virginia, you do not have to submit to a Preliminary Breath Test (PBT). The PBT is a small handheld breathalyzer machine that is a little bigger than a TV remote. It is carried by the police in the field and is administered on the roadside. By law, the

police officer must inform you that the results of the PBT test cannot be used at trial, and inform you that you have the right to see the results of the test.

Do not submit to a PBT. Even though a PBT may not be used at trial it can be used to justify arresting you and can be introduced at trial in some situations.

You also have a right to be offered a PBT if one is available. If you were stopped for DUI and the police never offered you a PBT test, the police may have violated your rights. In some situations, failure to offer a PBT may result in a DUI being dismissed. Notify your attorney immediately if you were never offered a PBT.

Do You Have to Use the ETD Breathalyzer?
The law requires you to submit to being tested by an Evidential Test Device (ETD) if you are arrested for DUI within three hours of driving on any public road. If you do not submit you will lose your right to drive for at least one year. However, refusal is not a criminal offense if you have never been convicted of DUI or refusal before.

ETDs are larger, more complicated breathalyzers that are used at the police station. They are about the size of a shoebox and have a keyboard and printer attached.

Before blowing into an ETD, the officer administering the breath test must observe you for 20 minutes. The breathalyzer operator should also inform you of your right to see the results and analysis of your test.

Refusal to submit to a breath test will result in a suspension of driving privileges for one year without an opportunity for a restricted driver's license. Being convicted of refusal to submit within ten years of being convicted of a DUI or a prior refusal to submit will result in a three-year suspension of the driver's license, up to six months in jail, and up to $1,000 in fines. If a person refuses to submit after two convictions of DUI or refusal (or a combination of the two) within the last ten years, he will lose his driving privileges for three years, will face up to 12 months in jail, and will be fined a maximum of $2,500.

Driving suspensions for DUI and refusal to submit will run back-to-back. A person who is convicted of his first DUI and first refusal to submit at the same time will lose his driving privileges for two years (one year for DUI and one year for refusal). A person with a prior DUI who is convicted of a second DUI and first refusal to submit will have his license suspended for six years (three for the second DUI and three for refusal to submit). Drivers convicted of refusal to submit cannot get a restricted license during the suspension period.

Do You Have to Give Blood?
If a driver is arrested for DUI and is suspected of being under the influence of drugs, or if he is physically incapable of giving a breath sample (because, for example, he has passed out or is in the hospital), the police may choose to take a blood sample in addition to or as a substitute for a breath test.

A driver who has been arrested for DUI has to submit to a blood test just as he must for a breath test. However, a driver must only submit if he has been *arrested*. Whether a driver is under arrest is not always clear, especially when a driver is in the hospital and is not placed in handcuffs or taken away. If in doubt, ask the police officer bluntly and clearly if you are under arrest. If you are not under arrest, you do not have to give them a blood sample.

The police do not have to offer the blood test as a substitute for the breath test. A driver can request a blood test, but the police do not have to give one. The police do not want to give blood tests because they take more time to process, are more difficult to administer correctly and trained personnel are not always available.

Do They Have to Show Me the Results of a Breath Test?

Police officers must allow you to see any digital results of any breath test, and they must also offer you a copy of any printout (if they exist). This rule applies to all breathalyzer machines, ETDs and PBTs. Additionally, the police officer administering the test must inform you of these rights before beginning the test.

Chapter 5:
"Did I Really Fail the Test?"
A Quick Guide to Field Sobriety Tests, PBTs, and
Breathalyzers

With the exception of sobriety checkpoints, the police
must see something wrong before they can pull you over.
If a police officer pulls a driver over without legal
justification, anything that officer discovers afterwards is
inadmissible in court.

Even after the police have pulled a driver over, the police
are limited as to what they can do. If the stop was for a
moving violation, the police can only detain the driver
long enough to run a background search and write a
ticket unless they discover evidence of another crime.

If a police officer wants to do more than write a ticket,
the officer needs evidence of intoxication to justify
further actions. Police officers must see erratic driving
(e.g., driving very slowly, straddling the line, hitting the
curve, and driving in the wrong lane), or, after pulling a
driver over, they must find other indicators such as:
glassy or blood shot eyes, slurred speech, the odor of
alcoholic beverage, open containers, or a lack of
coordination.

When an officer sees any combination of these things, he
or she may decide to ask you to step out of the car and
take a field sobriety test (FST) or blow into a preliminary
breath test (PBT). Both of these tests are voluntary.

66

Field Sobriety Test (FST)

FSTs are a series of exercises or tests used to determine sobriety. Most of the tests examine two things: 1) motor control/balance and 2) ability to follow instruction. Many of these tests are difficult and can easily be failed by a sober person. You are not required by law to submit to an FST.

In 1981 the National Highway Transportation Safety Administration (NHTSA) developed standardized field sobriety tests (SFST) to be used by law enforcement nationwide.

The three official NHTSA tests include very specific versions of the one-leg-stand, the nine-step-walk-and-turn, and the Horizontal Gaze Nystagmus (HGN) test. While the Standardized Field Sobriety Tests (SFST) developed by NHTSA are rigorously followed in many states, Virginia has no particular standards for administering FSTs.

The FSTs used by the police in Virginia vary between regions, jurisdictions, and individual officers. Often, officers use variations of the same test that may or may not resemble the NHTSA tests.

Some of the typical tests in Virginia include:
- The Walk and Turn (walk heel-to-toe on a straight line, then turn and walk back a specific number of steps);
- The One Leg Stand (stand on one leg without moving your arms and legs);

- Saying the alphabet, starting from a random letter and progressing forward;
- Counting backward between two given numbers;
- Touching your nose;
- Touching your thumb and fingers while counting;
- The Rhomberg Balance test (a.k.a. internal clock test) (close eyes, tilt head back, and stand still for 30 seconds); and
- The Horizontal Gaze Nystagmus test (HGN) (Following a pen or finger with just your eyes).

The Nine-Step-Walk-and-Turn

The "walk-and-turn" test has several variations in Virginia but usually involves an officer asking a driver to stand on a line (real or imaginary) with their right heel touching their left foot's toes while keeping their arms at their side.

While holding this position, the driver is given instructions on how to perform the test. After completing the instructions the officer tells the driver to begin. The driver then takes nine steps heel-to-toe along the line and then turns 180 degree and walks nine steps back.

During the test, the officer is looking for eight clues of intoxication.

1) Cannot maintain instructional position
2) Starts test too soon
3) Stops while walking

4) Not walking heel-to-toe
5) Steps off line
6) Uses arms for balance (raises them more than 6")
7) Loses balance on turn or turns incorrectly
8) Takes wrong number of steps

According to NHTSA, a driver must exhibit two of these eight clues in order to have "failed" the test. Virginia courts usually do not have any standardized definition of failure.

According to NHTSA, in order for this test to be accurate the ground where the test is performed must be dry, hard, level, non-slippery with sufficient room to maneuver. It cannot be too close to traffic as well. If you had to take this test under any of those conditions, notify your attorney immediately.

This test's validity is questionable if the driver is over 65 years old or has back, leg, or inner ear problems (or any medical issues that affect balance or muscle control). This test should not be performed in heels that are more than two inches high or in other footwear that makes it hard to balance (such as shape ups, flip flops, or perhaps even barefoot.)

Because this test measures a driver's ability to follow instructions, hearing impairment, mental or learning disabilities (such as dyslexia, autism, or ADD) and language barriers affect the accuracy of FSTs.

If there is anything that made your test extra difficult or if the test you performed was different from the one described above, tell your attorney immediately.

The One Leg Stand
The one leg stand begins with the driver standing at attention while the officer gives instructions. The driver is asked to lift one leg six inches off the ground while keeping his knees strait, arms at his side, and eyes on his elevated foot. The driver then counts "one one-thousand, two one-thousand" etc. until told to stop (usually after 30 seconds).

While there are several variations of this test in Virginia, normally the officers are looking for four clues of intoxication.

1) Sways while balancing
2) Uses arms to balance
3) Hopping
4) Puts foot down

NHTSA guidelines state that a person who exhibits two or more clues fails the test. In Virginia, most judges use their own experience and discretion to determine what is a failure.

The one leg stand should be performed on a dry, hard, level, and nonslippery surface. The driver should not be over 65 years old or more than 50 lbs overweight. He should not have back, knee, or inner ear problems, and should not be wearing more than two-inch heels.

Because this test measures a driver's ability to follow instructions, hearing impairment, mental or learning disabilities (such as dyslexia, autism, or ADD) and language barriers affect the accuracy of FSTs.

Weather conditions, traffic, distractions from the officer, and countless other things can also invalidate the results of the one leg stand test. Talk to your attorney about any conditions that made it hard for you to perform this test and tell your attorney if the officer's version of this test differed from the one described above.

Horizontal Gaze Nystagmus (HGN)
There is one FST that does not have anything to do with coordination and little to do with ability to follow instructions: the Horizontal Gaze Nystagmus (HGN) test.

Nystagmus is an uncontrollable tremor of the eye. All people have some nystagmus but intoxication causes it to become more readily observable in most people.
The HGN test involves an officer holding up a stimulus (a finger or a pen) in front of the driver's face while watching the driver's eye.

Before the HGN test begins the officer looks for nystagmus while the eyes are resting. The officer should also be looking to see whether the suspect's pupils are different sizes and whether either eye moves independently of the other. If the officer sees resting nystagmus, unequal pupil size, or independent movement, the HGN test is void and the suspect could be suffering from a serious medical condition.

To begin the HGN test, the officer has the driver hold their head still while following the officer's pen or finger with their eyes. The officer smoothly and slowly moves the pen or finger back and forth about 15 inches from the driver's face and slightly above their eye line.

First the officer looks to see whether the driver's eyes smoothly track the stimulus. Then the officer sees whether the driver's eye trembles while being held at the extreme left and right, and finally the officer looks for nystagmus when the eye is looking at less than a 45-degree angle.

Some officers look for "vertical nystagmus" as well. Vertical nystagmus is when the eye trembles as the driver looks to the extreme top of their field of vision.

According to NHTSA, the HGN is failed if the officer observes nystagmus in both eyes under the first two conditions (i.e. does not track smoothly, and nystagmus at the extreme left or right). If the driver exhibits nystagmus prior to 45 degrees or vertical nystagmus, it may be a sign of extreme intoxication or drug use.

A driver may exhibit nystagmus for several reasons other than intoxication. Some nystagmus is caused by medical conditions such as stroke, concussion and neurological disorders, to name a few. Other types of nystagmus are caused by officer error.

If the officer holds the stimulus too high it can create nystagmus (this is common when the driver is much shorter than the officer). Also, if the officer moves the pen too quickly back and forth, the driver will not track it smoothly.

If the test is administrated in a location where there are quickly moving objects within the driver's field of view (e.g. cars on the freeway), it may cause nystagmus. If an officer performs the HGN test repeatedly or takes too much time performing the test, the driver's eyes may become fatigued and exhibit nystagmus.

Because the correlation between intoxication and nystagmus is not something that the average person understands, some Virginia courts will not allow or give weight to HGN tests in a DUI trial. However, if you were given the HGN test make sure you talk to you attorney to determine whether the test was administered accurately and whether it may be used at trial.

Other Types of Field Sobriety Testing
Most officers administer at least one other test in addition to the "walk-and-turn", the "one leg stand" or the HGN test.

The alphabet test requires reciting the alphabet starting at one random letter and ending at another random letter. Drivers are instructed not to sing.

Prior to administering this test the officer should ask the driver what their level of education is and whether they are familiar with the English alphabet. Officers should never ask a driver to recite the alphabet backwards.

The finger dexterity test involves touching your thumb to your fingers in the same order as demonstrated by the officer (usually: pointer, middle, ring, pinky, pinky, ring, middle, pointer). The officer will often have the driver count out loud "1,2,3,4,4,3,2,1" while touching each finger.

Before giving the test, the officer should ask whether the driver has any medical conditions that affect their finger dexterity. The officer should also demonstrate the test.

 The Finger to Nose test is not just about finding your nose; it is also about following instructions. The officer will have the driver stand at attention with their arms straight out and say "left" and "right" in a specific order. At the officer's command, the driver takes their left or right hand and touches their nose with their pointer finger by bending at the elbow.

Unfortunately, this test can become very confusing if the officer is not clear about whether they mean their right or the driver's right. Additionally, the officer should inquire about medical conditions prior to beginning the test. Driver's with dyslexia may find it a challenge to keep their rights and lefts straight.

The Rhomberg test involves standing at attention with one's head tilted back and eyes closed. The driver may be asked to count to 30 while holding this position. The officer looks for swaying or trouble counting.

The officer should never ask the driver to count backwards while performing this test and the officer should inquire about medical conditions as well (legs, feet, back, inner ear, vertigo, etc.).

Because these tests measures a driver's ability to follow instructions, hearing impairment, mental or learning disabilities (such as dyslexia, autism, or ADD) and language barriers affect the accuracy of FSTs.

If an officer had you perform any of these tests differently than described above, or if you had a condition that affected your ability to perform these tests, tell your attorney immediately.

Preliminary Breath Test (PBT)

There are two types of breathalyzers used in Virginia: 1) the preliminary breath tester (PBT) and 2) the evidential test device (ETD). The biggest difference between these machines is that the PBT is voluntary. You have the right to refuse a PBT.

On the other hand, ETDs are usually mandatory if you have been arrested for DUI. You may be charged with refusal to submit to a breath test if you refuse to blow into an ETD.

PBTs are handheld devices that police officers use on the side of the road to determine a driver's blood alcohol content (BAC). PBTs are usually kept in the trunk of a police cruiser. They are small, portable machines with a plastic tube or mouthpiece that the driver blows into. PBTs can only be used to justify an arrest; they cannot be used as evidence at trial. PBTs are also completely voluntary.

A PBT: the Alco-Sensor III

PBTs are just machines, and, like all machines, they break. If a faulty PBT reading is used to arrest a driver, that arrest may be dismissed.

The PBT measures BAC with a fuel cell that mixes a sample of breath with a chemical called platinum phosphoric acid. The alcohol and chemical react to create an electrical charge. A voltammeter in the PBT measures how much electricity is created in order to calculate the driver's BAC.

While PBTs are very convenient, they are more susceptible to error than ETDs. Consequently, Virginia law states that the results of PBTs cannot be used against a driver in trial as proof of intoxication. Also, any driver may refuse to blow into a PBT and his refusal cannot be used as evidence of guilt.

However, if the driver voluntarily submits to taking a PBT, the police can use the PBT results as evidence that the driver was justifiably arrested for DUI. Do not agree to blow into a PBT.

Whenever the police stop a driver for DUI, they must inform the driver of certain rights regarding the PBT. 1) The driver has the right to see the BAC on the machine's readout. 2) The driver has the right to see the analysis of the BAC results. 3) The PBT cannot be used in trial as evidence of intoxication. 4) The driver can refuse to take the PBT without it being used against them. 5) Any driver suspected of DUI has the right to a PBT if such equipment is available.

If the officer did not inform you of all of these rights or if the officer did not offer you a PBT then talk to your attorney immediately.

In order to use a PBT for law enforcement, an officer must take certain steps to maintain the integrity of the PBT. 1) The officer must use an approved model of PBT; 2) they must use and maintain the PBT according to the manufacturer's instructions; and 3) the PBT must be properly calibrated.

The law requires the PBT to be used according to the manufacturer's instructions, but it is unfortunately quite common for those instructions to be ignored or forgotten by the police. For example, the Alco-sensor III must *not* be used if the machine's temperature is below 59° F / 15° C or above 96° F / 36° C. However, many officers keep their PBT in the trunk of their patrol car where the machine is either freezing cold or boiling hot.

Also, many PBTs are vulnerable to radio frequency interference (RFI) or radio signals from the police officers' communications devices. The radio signals strike the extremely sensitive voltammeter and cause sporadic readings. If the digital read-out flickers or the screen blanks instead of giving a reading it is a sign that the PBT is being influenced by RFI. If you see an officer using his radio near the PBT or having any of these problems, tell your attorney.

PBTs cannot distinguish between fumes from blood alcohol and fumes from mouth alcohol or stomach alcohol. The PBT will likely give a false high reading if a driver burps, vomits, or drank any alcohol within 20 minutes before testing.

Because PBTs ride around in the trunks of police cars all day, they need to be periodically tested and certified as accurate. There are guidelines for the regular calibration of PBTs and ETDs which an attorney may use to get a PBT result excluded from evidence.

Evidential Testing Devices (ETD)
Drivers who are arrested for DUI in the Commonwealth of Virginia are brought to the police station to have their breath tested with an Evidential Testing Device (ETD). All ETDs in the Commonwealth of Virginia are the same make and model: the INTOX EC/IR II.

Before testing a driver with the INTOX EC/IR II, the driver must be observed for at least 20 minutes. If he burps, vomits, or has anything in his mouth during the 20 minutes, the driver's mouth must be checked for foreign objects and the police must then observe him for another 20 minutes.

Before the breath test takes place, the officer administering the test must inform the driver that the driver has the right to observe the results of the test on the digital screen (not just on the print out).

Every driver tested in Virginia should exercise their right to see the results for themselves.

An ETD: the INTOX EC/IR II

When a driver is ready to take the ETD breath test, he will blow at least two times. The machine will print out the lesser of the two readings. If the machine detects any errors, an error screen will appear, and the machine will print out an error message that may be used as evidence of refusal to submit to a breath test.

The INTOX EC/IR II works the same way as the PBT with two noteable exceptions. First, while the PBT uses only an electrochemical (EC) process to determine BAC, the INTOX EC/IR II uses EC and infrared (IR) anaylsis processes to determine BAC.

IR anaylsis, called infrared spectroscopy, works by shooting infrared light of a specific wavelength that is absorbed by alcohol through a sample of breath. The infrared spectrometer measures how much of the light makes it through the sample. The less light that makes it through the breath sample, the greater the alcohol concentration of the sample. This process is used only to detect mouth alcohol errors while the electro chemical process generates the BAC reading.

The second difference between ETDs and PBTs is that the INTOX EC/IR II can also detect alcohol left over inside the machine or in the air around the machine. It can also run a limited self-diagnosis, and it will shut itself off if it detects certain specific errors. Despite all of these bells and whistles, the INTOX EC/IR II is still a machine and subject to errors.

The first potential for errors comes from the assumptions inherent in breathalyzer testing. All breathalyzers measure the concentration of alcohol in a person's breath and then use that measurement to estimate the blood alcohol concentration (BAC) of a person.

The BAC result displayed on the screen of any INTOX EC/IR II is just an estimation that is based on several assumptions: 1) that the driver's partition ratio is 2100:1; 2) that the driver's breath temperature is 34° C (93.2° F); 3) that the alcohol fumes in the driver's breath came from the lungs; and 4) that the driver's breath alcohol concentration is not affected by the volume of air exhaled.

The first assumption used by breathalyzers to estimate BAC is that the driver's partition ratio is 2100:1. The partition ratio is the ratio of blood alcohol to breath alcohol.

When a breathalyzer measures the alcohol concentration in a driver's breath, the breathalyzer multiplies that number by 2100 to calculate the driver's estimated Blood Alcohol Concentration (BAC).

The problem is that some driver's partition ratios are lower than 2100 at the time of testing. A lower partition ratio means the driver's estimated BAC will be higher than his actual BAC. For example: a driver with a partition ratio of 1842:1 and a real BAC of .07 will blow into a breathalyzer and produce an estimated BAC of .08.

Many things can cause a person to have a low partition ratio and thus a BAC result that is too high. Women generally have a lower partition ration than men. People with smaller lung capacity generally have lower partition rations. People with Chronic Obstructive Pulmonary Disease (COPD), asthma, lung disease or any condition that reduces lung volume will generally have lower partition ratios. If you have any conditions that affect your lung volume discuss them with your attorney.

The second assumption made by breathalyzers is that the driver's breath is always 34° C (93.2° F). Anyone who has watched a pot of water boil knows that the warmer a liquid gets, the more it evaporates (steams). Alcohol is the same. As the human body warms up, the percentage of alcohol vapors in the lungs rises, the partition ration decreases, and the estimated BAC results go up.

Because breathalyzers do not take a person's temperature, breathalyzers simply assume that everyone's breath temperature is 34° C (93.2° F). However, if the driver's breath temperature is over 34° C (93.2° F) the machine will return an erroneously high BAC reading.

It is estimated that a 1°C (1.8 ° F) increase in breath temperature will result in 6 to 8.5% increase in BAC results. So a person with a BAC of .07 and a breath temperature of 36° C (96.8° F) would blow a BAC of .08.

Consequently, if a person has a fever, is dressed too warm, or is left in a hot room too long, the breath test may be artificially high. If any of these conditions applied to you, talk to your attorney.

Another flaw with breathalyzers is that they assume all of the alcohol detected came from the driver's lungs. Alcohol fumes from a person's stomach, mouth, or throat are much more potent than the fumes from the lungs. A person that has recently consumed alcohol, burped, vomited or had any foreign object in their mouth may produce a BAC breath result that is too high.

Because of this problem, police officers in Virginia must check a driver's mouth and then "observe" the driver for 20 minutes before they administer a breath test at the police station. They are supposed to look for signs that the driver has burped, vomited, or put anything in his mouth in order to validate the results.

If you drank, vomited, burped or had anything in your mouth 20 minutes before taking a breath test, make sure you inform your attorney immediately.

The final flaw with breathalyzers is that they assume that a person's breath has the same alcohol concentrations no matter how the driver exhales. Studies have shown that BAC readings steadily climb the more a person exhales. Consequently, many officers aggressively encourage drivers to blow extremely long and hard into the machine in order to get the highest result possible.

Your attorney can obtain records to help determine whether your BAC involved an unnecessarily large breath sample. If your BAC was just a little bit above the legal limit or the elevated sentencing limits talk to your attorney about this defense. Because gathering these records can take several weeks, do not wait to retain an attorney.

Another weakness of these machines is that they are just machines. They break down and get old. That is why any ETD used in Virginia needs to be calibrated by the Department of Forensic Science (DFS) every six months or whenever it is repaired or altered. In order to introduce an ETD result into trial, the court may require breath technicians to produce evidence of regular maintenance and calibration of the machines.

Some breathalyzer results can also be erroneously influenced by Radio Frequency Interference (RFI) sources such as radios, cell phone, and power sources. If the breathalyzer operator or anyone near the machine was using a cell phone, radio, or other large electrical device talk to your attorney about what you observed.

Even if your BAC results were completely accurate there is one final flaw with breathalyzers in Virginia. Breathalyzers do not measure your BAC while you were driving.

The law in Virginia makes it a crime to *drive* with a BAC of .08 or more. However, if a driver's BAC is rising when they are arrested, that driver's BAC at the time of testing will be higher than it was when they were driving.

A person's BAC continues to rise for about one hour after drinking. If you were drinking less than one hour before you were pulled over, if your field sobriety tests and other behavior were above average, or if your PBT results were less than .08, your attorney made be able to argue that your BAC was below the legal limit when you were pulled over.

Blood Testing
If a driver is arrested for DUI and is suspected of being under the influence of drugs, or if he is physically

incapable of giving a breath sample (because, for example, he has passed out), the police may choose to take a blood sample in addition to or as a substitute for a breath test.

A driver who has been arrested is required by law to submit to a blood test just as he is for a breath test. However, a driver must only submit if he has been *arrested*. If a driver is in the hospital and the police have not arrested him for DUI, they must ask for permission to take a blood sample from the driver. If your blood was sampled without your permission, talk to your attorney immediately to determine when you were arrested and whether your rights were infringed upon.

Since 1995, the police do not have to offer the blood test as a substitute for the breath test. A driver can request a blood test, but the police do not have to give one. They often do not want to wait for the results of the blood test, which takes longer. Requesting a blood test is not a complete defense to being charged with refusal to submit to a breath test.

Blood tests, like breath tests, are regulated by Virginia law. If the police fail to comply with certain procedures and methods specified in law, the results of the blood test or the entire case may be dismissed.

When a driver baulks at submitting to a blood test the police must notify the driver that refusing to comply will result in a refusal to submit charge. They then must give the driver another opportunity to take the test.

The persons drawing the blood must be approved medical personnel. When blood is drawn at the police station, it must be contained in two separate vials supplied by the Department of Forensic Science (DFS). The vials must be sealed and accompanied by two completed certificates of withdrawal and must then be placed in a DFS-approved container and delivered to the officer.

The vials then go to DFS and are tested for alcoholic content via a method called "gas chromatography." Gas chromatography detects the amount of ethanol (the alcohol found in liquor) in blood by vaporizing the alcohol in a specific quantity of blood and then measuring the vaporized gas that escapes.

After the test is complete, a certificate of analysis is produced. The certificate must contain certain mandatory information about the driver, and it must be returned with the nurse's certificate of withdrawal to the court. Failure to return the certificate of analysis attached to the nurse's certificate of withdrawal may result in dismissal of the case.

The second vial is sent to DFS and is held for 90 days. The defense attorney can then have the vial sent to an independent laboratory for testing. If DFS loses the independent sample, the BAC results should be excluded from evidence. A good DUI attorney should always request independent testing, especially since the blood alcohol content of a sample tends to diminish after the blood is taken and the second test will often be lower.

Not all blood tests are done by law enforcement personnel. Sometimes hospitals run the blood test, especially when the driver is hospitalized due to an accident. Because the law allows the results of hospital blood analysis into trial, and because each hospital has a different process for drawing and testing blood, defense attorneys dealing with blood samples need to be aware of the varying methods used to test BAC. This fact is another reason to hire an attorney that specializes in DUI defense.

Typically, hospitals use the enzymatic method for determining BAC, but this method can be flawed because it tends to result in erroneously high readings if certain chemicals caused by tissue trauma are present in the blood (for instance, drivers who sustain bruises in an accident may give erroneously high BAC readings).

Blood-sample analysis is highly technical and requires an attorney who is not only experienced but is also familiar with the forensic science behind these complicated testing methods.

Chapter 6:
"Do I Have a Chance?"
Why Drivers Should Never Assume They Will Be Found Guilty.

If you have learned anything from this book, I hope you realize that DUIs are extremely complex. They are complicated to defend, but, more importantly, they are complex crimes to prosecute. DUIs are never as simple as they look, and a driver is always innocent until proven guilty.

In order to successfully prosecute DUIs, prosecutors, police, breath technicians, and the Department of Forensic Science personnel must all comply with strict and complex laws. There are dozens of ways that any one of these people can make a mistake that could affect the outcome of the case. Even if a mistake does not result in an acquittal, it may result in a lesser sentence.

The following sections lay out just a few of the many issues that may affect the outcome of your case. If any of these issues apply to you, make sure you discuss them with your attorney.

Jurisdictional Issues
Where a crime occurs dictates which courts can hear a case and which officers can arrest a driver. For example, a George Mason University police officer may not be able to stop and arrest a driver for DUI outside the boundaries of George Mason University and its abutting

roads. Also, the Prince William County General District Court may not hear a DUI case if the intoxicated driving did not occur within Prince William County.

Warrantless Arrests
For most DUI cases, if the officer does not personally witness a suspect driving, then the officer can only arrest the driver for DUI at the scene of an accident, at a hospital, or within three hours of driving. In many cases, if the officer cannot meet this burden then the case will be dismissed.

If an officer needs to prove that the arrest occurred within three hours of driving then the officer will need the defendant to admit when they were driving or the officer may need a witness who saw the defendant driving. This can make prosecution much more difficult.

If the arresting officer in your case did not personally witness you drive, then talk to your attorney about whether the arrest was valid.

Interacting with Multiple Officers
Typically there should only be one officer involved with a driver's stop, questioning, testing, search and arrest. We call that officer the arresting officer. Other officers may be present for backup, but those officers should have little or no interaction with the defendant.

The reason for this is simple. Officers can only testify to what the personally observed. If a backup officer interacts with a defendant and observes an important piece of evidence, then the backup officer may be required to come to court along with the arresting officer. If multiple officers are required, then prosecuting the case becomes more difficult.

If anyone but the arresting officer was involved in stopping you, questioning you, testing you, searching you or arresting you then talk to you attorney. If the second officer does not come to court then his evidence may not be admissible at trial.

Unconstitutional Traffic Stop
For most situations, in order to pull a driver over, an officer must have a "reasonable articulable suspicion" that a crime is occurring.

The officer must be able to articulate why they suspected that the driver had broken the law prior to pulling them over. Otherwise the court may declare the traffic stop unconstitutional and dismiss the entire case.

Vague accusations such as "he looked like he was speeding" or "he was driving drunk" may not be enough to justify a traffic stop.

Unconstitutional Arrest

In order to arrest a person for DUI, law enforcement officers must have "probable cause" that the driver was intoxicated and driving before they make an arrest. Without probable cause, the arrest is usually invalid and the DUI case may be dismissed. The court may also dismiss any refusal charge as well.

In order to justify an arrest, the prosecution will use four types of evidence in the following order: 1) PBT results, 2) Field Sobriety Test results, 3) driving behavior, and 4) other signs of intoxication (odor, slurred speech, blood shot eyes, lack of coordination, etc.).

Every driver accused of DUI should talk to their attorney about these four types of evidence and the possibility of having their arrest declared unconstitutional.

Drinking After Driving

Officers need to eliminate the possibility that a driver drank after they drove but before they were tested. If an officer finds an intoxicated driver anywhere but behind the wheel with the keys in the ignition, the officer will need to ask when the driver had their last drink and search the area thoroughly. Otherwise, proving the DUI will be difficult.

Intoxicated At the Time of the Offense (Rising BAC)
In Virginia, the government must prove that a driver was drunk at the time they were operating the vehicle not just when they were tested at the station.

If your PBT results at the scene were much lower than your BAC levels at the station, you may be able to prove that you were not legally intoxicated at the time you were pulled over.

This defense is particularly relevant when a person drank alcohol immediately before being pulled over. In that situation the alcohol in their stomach had not yet entered their blood stream at the time they were driving. Consequently, it may be argued that the driver would have arrived home or pulled over before becoming intoxicated had they not been arrested.

Operating a Vehicle
The police must prove that you were driving but they may also have to prove that you were driving within three hours of being arrested and/or tested.

If the police officer who arrested you did not personally witness you operating your vehicle there may be a good legal defense to your case. This situation is most common where the police respond to an accident or where the police found the driver sitting or sleeping in their car.

Field Sobriety Tests: Voluntariness

Field Sobriety Tests are completely voluntary. In Virginia, an officer is never allowed to force a driver to take an FST. If an office orders, forces, or pressures a driver into taking an FST then the court may find that the FSTs violated the driver's fourth amendment rights. The court may then exclude the FST from trial.

The Nine Step Walk and Turn & The One Leg Stand

In order for these tests to be accurate they must be administered correctly. Read chapter 5 for a more detailed description of how an officer should correctly administer these tests and point out any discrepancies to your attorney.

Both of these FSTs must be performed in an appropriate location. The ground must be flat, level, hard, non-slippery, clear of any debris, reasonably quiet, safe from traffic and other potential distractions or safety issues. Extreme weather can also affect these tests' accuracy.

Like other tests, both these tests check a driver's ability to follow instructions. Any language barriers, deafness, excessive noise, learning disabilities, mental retardation, developmental issues, etc. can possibility skew the outcome of this test.

If a driver has any problems balancing, walking, or standing then these tests may not be valid. Being over the age of 65, 50 pounds overweight, injuries to your back, legs, feet, knees, etc., inner ear problems, vertigo, clubbed feet, and arthritis are all examples of medical conditions that could affect this test. The driver should also be wearing appropriate footwear (no heels over two inches, flip flops or bare feet on gravel).

An officer should asked detailed questions about a driver's medical and physical condition prior to administering the tests in order to guarantee that these medical conditions are not present. Any time a driver is asked to perform either of these field tests after being in a serious accident, the results of these tests may be suspect.

Horizontal Gaze Nystagmus Test (HGN)
This test must be administered very precisely in order to be an accurate gauge of intoxication. If an officer moves the stimulus (their finger or a pen) too quickly (faster than one foot per second) it may cause a lack of smooth tracking. Holding the stimulus more than slightly above the eye line will also induce nystagmus. Making the driver hold their eyes at maximum deviation for too long or repeated testing can also lead to fatigue-induced nystagmus. Testing a driver while cars, emergency lights or other fast moving objects are within the driver's field of vision can also induce nystagmus.

Medical conditions, including injury from a car accident can cause nystagmus. An officer should check for resting nystagmus, equal tracking, and for equal pupil size prior to beginning the test to guard against these types of false positives.

This test is invalid if either of the driver's eyes moves independently of the other or if both eyes do not look in the same direction. If a driver was in an accident and had a concussion or stroke, then the HGN test may be invalid. If an officer sees nystagmus in one eye but not the other, the results of this test may be invalid.

The Alphabet Test
This test should never involve reciting the alphabet backwards. Additionally, this test is less reliable when the driver is not a native English speaker. The officer should ask the driver about their ability to read, write, and understand the English alphabet.

Testing in an extremely noisy environment can also cause the officer to hear errors that are not present. Shock from an accident, speech impediments, injuries to the lips or mouth, and an assortment of mental conditions including dyslexia and certain anxiety disorders can cause a driver to fail.

Finger Dexterity Test
Like other field sobriety tests, medical conditions, injuries, shock, language barriers, or any other condition that affect hand coordination or a driver's ability to follow instructions may invalidate this test. The officer

should ask about these medical conditions before beginning the test.

The officer should not combine this test with other tests or activities (e.g. the finger dexterity test combined with counting backwards). The officer should demonstrate this test in its entirety before asking the driver to begin.

Private Property
If a driver is arrested for DUI on a private road, parking lot, or driveway the government may be prevented from using or mentioning the breathalyzer results at trial. The legal issues surrounding arrests on private property are extremely complicated so talk to your attorney in detail if you believe that you were arrested for DUI on private property such as a parking lot, driveway, or private facility.

Preliminary Breath Tests (PBTs)
In order to arrest a driver for DUI, an officer must have "probable cause" to believe that the driver was committing DUI. Without probable cause, an officer cannot justify the arrest to a magistrate or judge and the case may be dismissed.

Preliminary Breath Tests (PBTs) cannot be used as evidence of intoxication for a conviction; however, a PBT can be used to justify an arrest. If a driver wants to invalidate an arrest for DUI, attacking the PBT may be essential.

In order to use a PBT to justify an arrest, the police must do four things: 1) they must use an approved brand and model of PBT; 2) they must use and maintain the PBT according to the manufacturer's instructions; 3) the PBT must be properly calibrated; and 4) the officer must inform the driver of his right regarding the PBT.

The law requires that the PBT be used according to the manufacturer's instructions. However, many officers ignore the manufacturer's instructions. For example, the Alco-sensor III must not be used if the machine's temperature is below 59° F / 15° C or above 96° F / 36° C. Despite this, many officers keep their PBT in the trunk of their patrol car where the machine is either freezing cold or boiling hot.

Also, many PBTs are vulnerable to radio frequency interference (RFI) or radio signals from police officers' radios and other electronic devices. The radio signals strike the extremely sensitive voltammeter and cause sporadic readings. Some signs that a PBT is being influenced by RFI are that the digital read-out flickers, the screen blanks instead of giving a reading, or the machine produces inconsistent samples. If you saw an officer using his radio near the PBT or if you saw any of these problems, tell your attorney.

Whenever the police stop a driver for DUI they must inform the driver of the following rights regarding the PBT. 1) The driver has the right to see the BAC results on the machine's readout. 2) The driver has the right to see the analysis of the BAC results. 3) The PBT cannot be used in trial as evidence of intoxication. 4) The driver can refuse to take the PBT without their refusal being used against them. 5) They have a right to a PBT if such equipment is available.

If the officer in your case did not inform you or these rights or did not offer you a PBT test, talk to your attorney about the possibility of getting the PBT excluded or the arrest dismissed.

Not Tested Within Three Hours of Driving
The police have no right to test a driver more than three hours after they last drove. If the time on your BAC certificate is more than three hours after you were driving, then your breath test results may be inadmissible in court. Tell you attorney immediately.

Mouth Alcohol: Burping and Other Issues
Evidentiary Testing Devices (ETDs) assume that all the alcohol fumes they detect came from the driver's lungs. Alcohol fumes from a person's stomach, mouth, or throat are much more potent than the fumes from their lungs. A person who has recently consumed alcohol, burped, or vomited will produce a BAC breath result that is higher than normal.

Because of this problem, police officers in Virginia must observe the driver for 20 minutes before administering the breath test at the police station. During those 20 minutes, the breath test operator is supposed to look for signs that the driver has burped, placed anything in his mouth, or vomited. The officer administering the ETD breath test should request that the driver not burp, vomit, or place anything in his mouth before taking the test.

If the driver burps, vomits, or has anything in his mouth, the driver's mouth must be cleaned out and the driver must be observed for another 20 minutes before testing. This procedure is extremely important. However, not all operators consistently monitor drivers.

If the operator did not monitor you for the full 20 minutes or if you burped, vomited, regurgitated hiccupped, or had anything in your mouth prior to testing, notify your attorney immediately.

Acid Reflux, Chronic Heartburn, GURDS, Gastric Bypass and Other Medical Conditions

As mentioned above a breath test may be artificially high anytime stomach fumes escape into the airways. This condition can occur frequently and without "burping" in people with acid reflux, chronic heartburn, GURDS, gastric bypass surgery, or similar conditions. Therefore, breath test results in people with these conditions may be artificially high.

Make sure your attorney knows your relevant medical history if you have any of these, or similar, conditions.

Diabetes, Low Carb Diets, and Irritable Bowel Syndrome

In certain situations the body produces alcohol. Your body's alcohol by itself or in combination with liquor may cause an artificially high reading.

Diabetics suffering from hyperglycemia will create a form of alcohol in their bodies that will give their breath an odor similar to sweet wine. This medical condition can cause erroneous BAC readings. In extreme situations hyperglycemia can also cause slurred speech, loss of coordination, confusion and loss of consciousness.

Non-diabetics' bodies may also produce their own alcohol when on aggressive low carb diets. As their body breaks down the fats in their bodies, the body excretes isopropyl alcohol in the breath and urine. Drivers with this condition will often notice a distinct change in the smell of their breath similar to that of diabetics.

Irritable bowel syndrome may, in some situations, cause the bowels to become a micro-brewery that can affect BAC results. If any of these conditions apply to you, talk to your attorney about your medical history immediately.

Breath Temperature

Because the breathalyzer machines do not take a person's temperature, the breathalyzers simply assume the driver's breath temperature is 93.2° Fahrenheit (34° C) when it calculates the BAC. However, if the driver's body temperature is over 93.2° F (34° C) the machine will return an erroneously high BAC reading.

If a driver has a fever, is dressed too warm, or is left in a hot police car too long, their breath test may be erroneously high. Talk to your attorney if your core temperature was above average during testing.

Deep Breaths/Blowing Too Hard
The more air a person blows into a breathalyzer machine, the higher the BAC results tend to be. Additionally, drivers who take a big breath and hold it before blowing into a breathalyzer will increase the BAC reading, while drivers who hyperventilate will decrease the BAC results.

For these reasons, the police want you to inhale a great big breath and then blow really hard, so that your BAC results will be as high as possible. Often, an officer will stand over a driver and yell at him to blow harder. Erroneously high BAC readings may result from being forced to blow extremely hard and long.

Blowing too hard can also invalidate a sample. If officers are forcing a driver to blow really hard into the machine, the machine may repeatedly produce an "invalid sample" reading. If the officer does not understand why the machine is producing an "invalid sample" reading they may assume the driver is playing games with the machine and charge the driver with refusal to submit.

If you were instructed to take a great big breath and blow extremely hard into the machine, talk to your attorney about potential defenses.

COPD, Asthma, Lung Disease, and Other Conditions

Breathalyzers do not actually measure a person's blood alcohol content (BAC), they only *estimate* the BAC by measuring the amount of alcohol in a person's breath. To estimate BAC based on breath alcohol, the breathalyzer uses a conversion number called a "partition ratio". The breathalyzer will multiply the driver's breath alcohol concentration by the partition ratio in order to estimate their blood alcohol concentration.

Because the breathalyzers do not measure each individual's true partition ratio, the machine assumes the same partition ratio for every person. The partition ratio used in Virginia is 2100:1.

If a driver has a partition ratio of less than 2100 then their estimated BAC will be erroneously high. A driver with an actual BAC of .06 and a partition ratio of 1500:1 will produce an estimated BAC reading of .08 when they blow into a breathalyzer.

Any condition that reduces lung volume may cause a person's partition ratio to be lower than 2100. Asthma, COPD, lung diseases, are just a few of the conditions that may cause a driver's estimated BAC to be too high. Talk to your attorney about your medical history if similar conditions apply to you.

Gender

As mentioned above, having a low partition ratio means that your BAC test results will be too high. Many women have much lower partition ratios than men and thus most women will produce higher BAC results than men.

Machine Errors

There are many things that can interfere with a breathalyzer's ability to take an accurate reading. While ETDs are much less susceptible to errors than PBTs, both suffer from the same potential problems.

Some typical machine errors include radio frequency interference (RFI), where radio signals from the officers' communication devices strike the extremely sensitive voltammeter in the ETD or PBT. RFI can cause sporadic BAC readings. Officers should not use cell phones, radios, or other electronic devices near a breathalyzer while a test is in progress. If you see anyone using electronic devices during your breath test, talk to your attorney immediately.

One More Chance

Before a driver is charged with refusal to submit to a test, the officer must read a standardized form to the driver which explains the consequences of refusal. Then the officer must give the driver one more chance to take the test after reading the form.

If an officer charges a driver for refusal without reading them the consequences of refusal or if the officer did not give them one more chance after reading the form, then the refusal charge and the DUI charges may be dismissed.

Bruises/Body Trauma

Blood samples taken at the hospital are often the key piece of evidence in a suspected DUI-related accident. Typically, hospitals use the enzymatic method for determining BAC, but this method may result in erroneously high readings that confuse the byproducts of tissue trauma with ethyl alcohol. This means that drivers who sustain serious tissue injuries in an accident may be falsely accused of being intoxicated if tested by the enzymatic method.

Chapter 7:
"Do I Really Need an Attorney?"
The Top Ten Reasons to Hire an Attorney

1. They Pay for Themselves

When people say they don't want an attorney, what they are usually saying is: "I don't want to *pay* for an attorney." Who can blame them? We all have things we would rather spend our money on.

However, if you are arrested for DUI, hiring an attorney is worth it. The true cost of a DUI conviction is staggering, and if your attorney can reduce even some of those consequences then they are worth every penny.

A first DUI conviction may cost a driver thousands of dollars. A driver convicted of a single DUI may pay up to $2,500 in fines, but may also have to pay for ASAP registration fees, mandatory drug and/or alcohol treatment (which can cost thousands more in some situations), license reinstatement fees, restricted license fees, structured payment fees, interlock installation and rental fees, impoundment fees, court services fees, driver improvement class fees, and, of course massive insurance premiums that may last for years. All of this does not include the consequences of losing your license for 12 months or going to jail.

For some drivers, a serious criminal conviction may cost them their job or hurt their chances of getting into an academic program.

A DUI can also affect immigration status, particularly if the immigrant has Temporary Protective Status (TPS). Undocumented aliens will likely be identified by ICE agents and deported from jail if they serve even one day in jail.

A DUI conviction can affect a person's security clearance and background checks. Colleges, law schools, state bars, medical schools, the military, government employers, life insurance providers and government contractors are just some of the institutions that check their applicants' criminal histories.

An untimely DUI conviction may hurt a parent's child-custody rights. A criminal charge, especially one that involves substance abuse, is never helpful when child-custody issues are at stake. It can be hard to argue for custody of a child if a parent cannot drive their child anywhere.

Of course, one of the biggest problems with a DUI conviction is jail time (up to 12 months for the first DUI conviction). Drivers with BAC levels at .15 or higher can expect mandatory jail. For subsequent DUI convictions things are many times worse.

Loss of license and mandatory jail time can be much longer if you have been convicted of a DUI in the last 5 or 10 years. Fines are higher, costs are higher, and insurance premiums are much higher.

Attorneys cost money, but your DUI trial is not the time to cut corners.

2. Being Innocent is Not Enough

If you believe you are innocent you absolutely need an attorney. The rights and defenses mentioned in this book may be lost completely unless they are presented to the court at the right time and in the right format.

Unless you have a DUI attorney who understands the complex rules of evidence and procedure, the court may never even discuss the many legal issues contained in this book. It is not enough to be right, you must know how and when to exercise your rights or those opportunities may be lost forever.

3. Lone Defendants Are Treated Differently

Some jurisdictions do not provide unrepresented defendants with the opportunities to negotiate a plea. Not having an opportunity to negotiate a plea is a massive disadvantage. By having an opportunity to negotiate, the represented driver has double the opportunities for someone to sympathize and double the chances of having their case assigned to someone who will treat them favorably.

Beside negotiation opportunities, almost every jurisdiction gives represented defendants scheduling preference on the day of trial. This means that the judge calls your case only when your attorney is ready instead of whenever your file appears on the judge's desk. In those jurisdictions a driver without an attorney cannot be late to court, cannot step out to go to the bathroom, and cannot go to check the parking meter for fear of their case being called while they are gone. Having an attorney means that there is less stress and fewer opportunities for things to go wrong on the day of your trial.

4. You Never Know What Kind of Case You Have Until It Is Too Late

Some people do not get an attorney because they think there is nothing an attorney can do for them. Do not be fooled; DUI cases are extremely complicated and difficult to prosecute. There is no way to know what kind of case you have unless you have spoken to a competent DUI attorney. There is no reason to not get a free consultation.

5. Not Everything Is Innocent Versus Guilty

Even if you just want to show up to trial and plead guilty, you need an attorney. The sentencing portion of a DUI case can be very complicated. There are around 17 different punishments that are associated with a DUI conviction, and the judge has a lot of control over how severe these punishments can be.

The commonwealth attorney or judge can also amend a DUI to one of several lesser offenses based for any number of reasons. BACs can also be lowered at the Commonwealth's discretion and a previous DUI conviction can be voluntarily excluded from trial. Any one of these decisions would have extreme effects on the punishment you receive.

Even though a drunk driver may be found guilty, the number of different outcomes is immeasurable. It takes a good attorney to not only negotiate a fair punishment, but also to explain the many different consequences so that the client can make informed decisions.

6. Do Not Enter the Red-Tape Jungle Alone

Where and how do you get a restricted license? How do you get your license back? Can you sign up for weekend jail time or work release? Where and when do you register for ASAP? What happens if you are sick and miss your court date? What do you do if you get a traffic ticket while on probation? How do you change your ASAP schedule? How do you amend your restricted license?

I could write one hundred pages filled with the questions people ask when they enter Virginia's judicial system. The sheer amount of paperwork and bureaucracy involved in a simple DUI is staggering. Do not enter the red-tape jungle without a guide. You may never been seen again.

Red tape is not only frustrating and tedious; it can also get you arrested. One thing a good attorney can do is help you comply with probation. DUI convictions usually come with a lot of suspended jail time and fines. This means that if you fail to turn in all of your paperwork, comply with ASAP, pay all of your fines, and stay out of trouble, then you risk going to jail and paying extra fines.

The law is not very forgiving. If you do not have an attorney, the odds of ending up in jail on a probation violation are higher. I have seen plenty of drivers go to jail because they tried to take care of their probation requirements themselves and promptly got arrested.

Make sure that you have an attorney that will walk you through the post-trial paperwork and not just represent you at trial.

7. Pre-Trial Preparation Is a Pain

A good DUI attorney may work on a DUI case for several months but will only spend a few hours in court. The vast majority of the work is dealing with the court procedures before trial, paperwork, and the general pains that come from working with a massive bureaucracy.

When people hire an attorney, they often feel like the attorney is getting paid to stand up in court and talk. The truth is that the vast majority of your attorney's time is spent gathering evidence, filling out forms and making sure the paperwork is filed correctly.

If you show up to trial without taking care of the paper work, you may have lost the battle before you ever open your mouth. You do not want to wait until the day of your trial to find out whether everything was filed correctly. A good DUI attorney will take care of the preparation work for you.

8. Known Unknowns

Inevitably, there is always someone who will read this book and say, "I can do that—I do not need to hire an attorney." This book should serve as a warning to show you how many unknown factors exist. Do not let the legal resources in this book and on the internet lull you into believing this process is easy.

9. You Have Better Things to Do

Even if a defendant were capable of representing himself, he should ask whether he wants to spend the next few months dealing with his DUI or taking care of his life. Between work and family, the DUI defendant is also dealing with preparing for the possibility of losing his driver's license, going to jail, or even losing his job. Do you want to spend that time trying to figure out how the court system works as well?

A good attorney not only makes good financial and strategic sense, but it is an enormous emotional relief during a very stressful time. It can be invaluable to know that someone you trust is taking care of your case while you take care of the rest of your life. If I were ever arrested, the first thing I would do is call an attorney.

10.   Court Appointed Attorneys: Pros and Cons.

Many people ask me about hiring their own attorney as opposed to applying for a court-appointed attorney. However, most people do not qualify for a court appointed attorney.

Only the poor (or indigent) are provided with a free attorney. In order to be declared indigent in the Commonwealth of Virginia, you must make less than or equal to 125% of the federal poverty line. The federal poverty line is adjusted by how many people are in your family. The poverty line for 1 person is $9,800. For 2 people, it is $13,200. For 3, it is $16,600. For 4, the line is $20,000. Hence, if the defendant has a family of four with an income of more than $25,000 ($20,000 x 1.25), that defendant is too rich to get a court-appointed attorney (*check with the court for the most up-to-date financial guidelines*).

Chapter 8:
"How Do I Hire an Attorney?"
A Guide to Attorney-Client Contracts and the Retention Process.

It is important to hire an attorney *immediately* if you are ever charged with a crime. However, it is even more important if that crime is a DUI. Most people do not realize that some of the defenses to DUI expire long before trial. If you do not have an attorney to file specific paperwork before the expiration date, you lose the chance to make those defenses. Never put off hiring an attorney.

Besides, you usually pay the same amount for an attorney no matter when you hire them. Why not get more service for your money by hiring your attorney sooner?

Getting a Continuance to Hire an Attorney
If your trial date is approaching and you still do not have an attorney, most courts will allow you one or two continuances in order to find representation. However, using continuances for this purpose can be dangerous. In addition to losing the opportunity to make certain defenses, you may also lose the right to make future continuances. You are allowed a limited number of continuances. If you use all of your continuances finding an attorney, then you will not have any left for trial.

Continuances are very important and should never be wasted. Continuances can be used to discover what evidence the prosecution has against you. In many jurisdictions, your attorney cannot talk to the police or commonwealth attorney to discover their evidence against you until the actual day of trial. When your attorney cannot see the evidence against you until the day of trial then continuances are needed in order to prepare a defense.

Also, being granted continuances may increase the odds that the court will grant the prosecuting attorneys a continuance if they ask for it. If the police officer or breathalyzer operator does not show up at trial, the prosecution will likely ask for a continuance in order to prevent the case from being dismissed. However, if the court has already granted you several continuances, the court may be more likely to grant the Commonwealth a continuance as well.

Do not put yourself in a position where you or your attorney will have to waste continuances. Find an attorney immediately.

Typical Fee Structures
Most (but not all) criminal defense attorneys in Virginia charge a flat fee and demand that the fee be paid before they agree to represent you.

These fees usually do not cover any court expenses (such as hiring a court reporter, gathering evidence, serving process, or hiring expert witnesses). Court reporters and process servers can cost hundreds of dollars while expert witnesses can cost thousands of extra dollars. Discuss the possibility of needing these services before you sign an attorney-client contract.

Some attorneys also have different rates for appeals, certain motions, continuances, going to trial versus taking a plea, jury trial versus a trial without a jury. It is very important to read the fine print of your attorney-client contract and discuss the possibility of being charged for these extra expenses.

Post-Trial Services
Some attorney-client contracts end as soon as the judge makes a ruling. When those drivers walk out of the courtroom, they no longer have an attorney. In this situation the attorney may not be obligated to aid the client in registering for the mandatory Alcohol Safety Action Program (ASAP), applying for a restricted license, getting their bail back, paying fines, or appealing their conviction.

If you are convicted of DUI there is a significant chance that you could be sentenced to additional jail time if you fail to comply with ASAP, the terms of your restricted license, or other conditions imposed by the judge. An attorney can be invaluable in helping you navigate the post-conviction process. Always make sure your retention agreement defines post-conviction responsibilities.

Beginning and Ending an Attorney-Client Relationship

It is extremely important for the attorney and the client to clearly define how and when their relationship will begin and end. It is also important to define what conditions will terminate an agreement. Can your attorney drop you as a client? Can you switch attorneys if you are not satisfied? If you terminate the agreement will your money be refunded? What happens if your attorney becomes sick or otherwise unavailable? These questions should be clearly addressed in the retention agreement.

Orders of Substitution

If you ever want to change attorneys, your new attorney must file an order of substitution with the court; however, the motion for an order of substitution requires the signature of the old attorney, the new attorney, the defendant and in some cases it also requires the signature of the prosecution. This process can take quite a bit of time so if you are not satisfied with your attorney, do not wait to find a new one.

Chapter 9:
"How Do I Find a Good DUI Attorney?"
How to Spot a Bad Attorney and What to Look for in a
Good One

Picking the right attorney for you and your case is a very
personal decision. While there is no formula to finding
the perfect attorney, this chapter is a list of things to
consider while you are looking for an attorney.

Get a Free Consultation and Use It Effectively
Almost every criminal defense attorney offers a free
consultation (by phone or in person). Use the
consultation to get to know your attorney. Before
meeting with an attorney make a list of questions you
have for them and write down the important details about
your case.

Read the Contract Carefully
The attorney you hire is only as good as the contract you
sign. The retention agreement will spell out what the
attorney will and will not do for you.

Make sure the attorney you hire will walk you through
the very complicated post-conviction processes and take
your case to appeal if needed. Some drivers who attempt
to navigate the post-trial process without an attorney end
up getting arrested because they did not understand what
the law required them to do. Remember, it does not

matter how good an attorney is if the contract does not require them to help you.

What Is Your Attorney's Focus Areas?

There are many different areas of law that a lawyer can practice but only so many hours in the day that an attorney can spend studying DUI legal and forensic issues. Have a frank and open discussion about how many DUI cases your attorney does on a regular basis. Talk to your attorney about what they do to increase and update their knowledge of DUI law and forensic issues.

Because DUI law is so complicated and because DUI laws changes so frequently, it can be essential to hire an attorney who invests substantial time and resources learning about DUI law.

Who Will Be Working on Your Case?

Sometimes the attorney who interviews you is not the attorney that represents you at trial. Have a frank discussion about how your case will be delegated and who is going to be representing you at court.

Having multiple attorneys working on your case can be a good thing. However, make sure you understand what each attorney's role will be and if possible, interview all attorneys who will be working on your case before signing a contract.

Does Your Attorney Have Enough Time?

Most of the mistakes made by attorneys happen because those attorneys are too busy, not because they are inexperienced or incompetent. Your attorney needs to have all the facts about the case and understand how the various consequences of a DUI will affect you. There is no substitute for spending time talking with your attorney. If you do not feel like you have had enough time to talk, get another attorney.

Do I Trust My Attorney?

Because most of a DUI defense happens outside the courtroom, most of what an attorney does is done behind closed doors. You cannot watch your attorney 24/7 and you should never feel you must micromanage your attorney. If you do not feel comfortable trusting your attorney with your case you should get another attorney.

Does Your Attorney Empower You?

An attorney is a counselor, not a ruler. The attorney's job is to explain the options and consequences to the client and thus empower the client to make informed decisions. Empowering a client to make informed decisions about what to plead, what deals to take or reject etc., is a process that begins at the very first meeting.

Make sure you hire an attorney who you feel is doing a good job listening, asking questions, and explaining. Once again, there is no substitute for spending time talking to your attorney.

Does Your Attorney Care?

The second biggest complaint I hear from defendants is that their attorney does not care. Criminal defense can be a very emotionally demanding profession. It can be difficult to constantly empathize with what your clients are going through.

If you feel your attorney is not concerned about your problems, hire another attorney.

What is Their Experience?

When it comes to experience, it is quality, not quantity that matters. It is not a bad idea to find out how much experience they have with your type of case. How much experience do they have in your jurisdiction? How will their particular experiences affect their ability to represent you? It may also be informative to talk to your attorney about what aspects of your case would be new for them.

Is Your Lawyer Detail Oriented?

When it comes to criminal defense, the devil is in the details. I saw this first hand as a new attorney when I watched a driver go to jail for five days simply because his defense attorney did not notice a typo on the plea agreement. As the bailiff dragged the confused and terrified man to jail, the judge told the attorney that they should have read the agreement more carefully. You *do not want this to happen to you!*

Use the free consultation period to gauge how detail-oriented your attorney is. I am also a firm believer that how attorneys take care of themselves and their offices says a lot about how detail-oriented they are in their profession as well.

Hire the Best Attorney You Can Afford.
Try to keep price comparisons in perspective when shopping for an attorney. Do not make the mistake of hiring your second choice just to save a few dollars.

Also, always compare fee structures as well as services. Will your attorney do the appeal for free or will they charge you? Is there a different fee for trials versus pleas? Is there a fee for jury trial? Is there a fee if the case goes beyond a preliminary hearing? It is usually a good idea to budget for the possibility of a trial and an appeal.

If the attorney who is the best fit for you is out of your price range do not give up. Have an open and honest discussion with that attorney about your financial situation. Some attorneys may choose to offer payment plans or pro bono services.

People Skills Are Important
Before you go to trial, your attorney will have a chance to talk the prosecution into giving you what you want. At trial, your attorney will try to get the judge to give you what you want. Trials and plea negotiations are all about people skills.

The best attorneys are friendly, confident, and assertive. They can demand respect while treating others respectfully. If an attorney bad-mouths the judges, prosecutors, or other attorneys, odds are that those same people are bad-mouthing him.

Is My Attorney Honest and Ethical?
The courts in Virginia have long memories, and a lawyer who is not trusted may be a detriment to your case. Additionally, you will be placing a large amount of trust in the person you hire to represent you.

Look for those attorneys who have the highest ethical and moral standards. If you have doubts about the integrity of your counselor, consider looking elsewhere.

"Chapter 10:
"How Do I Get Out of Here?"
Being Arrested, Making Bail, and Getting Your Car out of Impound

Custody versus Summons
After being arrested in Virginia, you will either be taken to jail or released on a summons. (A summons is a piece of paper instructing you when and where to appear in court.) Generally, if a driver is arrested for DUI, the police will take the driver to the police station or jail for additional testing and then take them into custody.

Magistrates
A person who is arrested and taken into custody for DUI will typically appear before a magistrate. Magistrates perform two jobs: 1) the magistrate verifies that the police officer had probable cause to arrest the suspect, and 2) the magistrate sets bail.

In order to administratively suspend a driver's license the arresting officer will sign a statement of the facts called a criminal complaint and deliver it to the magistrate. A few days after the arrest, a copy of the criminal complaint can be obtained at the court clerk's office.

The magistrate will also issue an arrest warrant and set bail. If a magistrate gives you a high bond or no bond, your attorney can file a bond motion. A bonds motion is a request for a General District Court (GDC) judge to reconsider the issue of bond. If the GDC judge refuses, the attorney can appeal to the Circuit Court. Each appeal requires at least one business day to file.

If the magistrate does not require the driver to pay a bond then the driver will be release as soon as they sober up.

Intake

When a driver is arrested and taken to jail they go through an intake process. The medical staff examines them, their property may be taken and inventoried, and they are finger printed and photographed.

The intake process can produce important evidence in a DUI trial. The intake photograph can be used to refute an officer's accusation that a driver had glassy bloodshot eyes or that they looked extremely intoxicated.

Documentation from the medical intake examination can be used to establish the presence of injuries that affected the driver's ability to perform field sobriety tests. Keep any documentation given to you at the jail and show it to your attorney as soon as possible.

Contacting Your Attorney

Defendants may get their first chance to call an attorney when they are in jail. Most of the jails in Virginia have telephone access, and the inmates can make collect calls. Most attorneys will accept collect calls from clients. Some jails allow free calls to attorneys who registered with the jail.

Bail

Bail is set by the magistrate and is based on two factors:
1) the likelihood of the defendant showing up on the trial
date, and 2) the risk to the public if the defendant is
released from jail.

The magistrate will look at whether the defendant has
ever been charged with failure to appear in court, the
severity of the charges, past criminal record, and the
driver's ties to the community. Drivers who are arrested
while already on bond or probation have more trouble
getting bond than others.

If a magistrate sets an excessively high bail or if the
magistrate does not provide you with bail then your
attorney can file a bond motion and ask a GDC or Circuit
Court judge to set bond with little or no bail.

Bail Bondsman

Bail bondsmen will, for a fee, post your bond for you and
can usually expedite your release on bond. Bail
bondsmen charge a fee of approximately 10% of the
bond to bail someone out of jail. For some bonds, they
may also require a cosigner who will pay them back if
the defendant does not show up to court. Bail bondsmen
will also usually accept collect calls from jail.

Impound/Park/Other Driver

When someone is arrested for DUI the police can
impound the car if it is not parked in a legitimate parking
spot. Sometimes, if the police officer is in a good mood
and there is a sober, licensed driver nearby, the officer

may allow the sober driver to move the car. The police will usually not park your car for you.

If the car is towed and impounded, it may cost approximately $120 plus $60 per day. The police may also do a limited search of the car if it is impounded.

If you drove on a revoked license and your car was impounded, your attorney may be able to get the car out of impound, especially if someone else's name is on the title or if he can get the arrest dismissed. If there was no probable cause for the arrest, your attorney may be able to get the impound fees reimbursed.

ICE Detainers

For foreigners, being arrested is a particularly terrible experience no matter what documentation you have. Many counties in Virginia aggressively try to deport aliens who are arrested. If an alien is arrested in Virginia, the Immigration and Customs Enforcement (ICE) agents may interview the inmate to determine their status in this country.

If there is any delay in establishing an alien's status in this country or if they are here illegally, an ICE agent may place an ICE detainer on that inmate. ICE detainers are orders requesting the sheriff's department to hold the inmate in jail until ICE can come and get him. ICE detainers are the first step in deportation.

If you are an alien and are arrested in Virginia, post bail and contact an attorney as soon as physically possible. If an alien can post bail fast enough, they may get released before ICE gets involved. If you are an alien and have been arrested, the worst thing you can do is procrastinate calling an attorney.

Chapter 11:
"What Do I Need to Do to Prepare for Trial?"
How to Get the Most out of Your Attorney.

Get an Attorney as Soon as Possible
If you are arrested for DUI or refusal to submit to a breath test, get the best attorney you can afford *as soon as possible*! You have several defenses and key rights that may expire as early as 14 days after being arrested. Without an attorney, you may lose those rights.

An attorney may also help you get your license back, get your car back, or get you a pretrial restricted license. You are likely going to pay the same price for an attorney no matter when you hire one, so you might as well hire one as soon as possible. Doing so will allow you to get the most for your money.

Proving Innocence and Mitigating Damages
There are two types of evidence: 1) evidence that proves innocence and 2) mitigating evidence that proves you deserve a less severe sentence. Whether you are innocent or not, you need to gather both types of evidence.

Write Down Everything
As soon as you are arrested, write down all the details that you can remember. In Virginia, the prosecution may not have to notify your defense attorney about the evidence it has against you before trial. Additionally, many law enforcement agencies in Virginia do not have

cameras in their police cruisers. Therefore, your attorney's most important source of information is you.

The most important details involve the conversations you had with the police. What questions did they ask you? What did you say to them? Did they read you your rights? Write down as much information as you can, as soon as you can.

Gathering Documents
Do not procrastinate gathering evidence. Most documents used in court should be originals or certified copies. These documents take time to gather. An attorney can help you with this process so do not put off getting an attorney in order to gather evidence.

Some documents you will want include a copy of the criminal complaint (found at the court clerk's office) and a copy of your DMV records from all the states that have issued you a driver's license in the last five years.

Other important documents include accident reports, accident photos, and also, documentation of any drug or alcohol treatment programs. Also make sure to keep all the documents you received at the jail and get them to your attorney as soon as possible.

Register for ASAP
Registering for ASAP before trial may make getting a restricted license easier. If a driver is likely to be convicted of DUI or "wet reckless", registering for ASAP before the trial may allow you to get a restricted license

sooner. Some judges will only grant a restricted license after the driver has been evaluated by ASAP. So preregistering can reduce the amount of time you spend unable to drive to and from work.

Each ASAP program is tailored to the individual driver. Drivers who have multiple DUIs or substance abuse issues may be required by ASAP to attend more rigorous and more expensive programs in addition to ASAP.

Preregistering for ASAP will give the drive a better understanding of what ASAP will require. If you are not sure whether to plead guilty or go to trial, understanding what ASAP will require you to do will make the decision easier. Drivers who preregister for ASAP, but then win at trial, can quit ASAP at any time.

Register for AA or Rehabilitation
Drivers who may suffer from a substance abuse problem should consider beginning to attend AA or a similar drug or alcohol treatment program before trial. Your attendance in one of these programs can be kept quiet if you are found innocent, and it may be presented to the court as mitigating evidence if you are found guilty.

Defensive Driving Classes
Attending defensive driving classes can restore up to five points to your Virginia driver's license. It may encourage a judge or prosecutor to give you a more lenient sentence if you have a bad record or have been charged with traffic offenses in addition to DUI.

Restitution

If a DUI results in an injury or destruction of property, the driver, under the supervision of his attorney, may want to pay restitution to the other party before trial in order to increase the likelihood of a reduced sentence. However, make sure you consult your attorney first.

Fill Out the Restricted Operators License Application

If you want to be given a restricted operator's license, fill out the form with your attorney prior to trial. This form must be completed and signed by the judge at trial if you want to be issued a restricted license immediately. Putting it off or filling it out at the last minute can result in serious problems. The restricted operator's license form can be found online on the Virginia Supreme Court's website.

Prepare for the Worst-Case Scenario

Make sure that you are ready for the worst-case scenario on the day of trial. Take the entire trial day off from work unless your attorney says otherwise. Do not drive yourself to the courthouse if there is a chance that you will be found guilty that day. If you are found guilty and lose your license or are sentenced to jail, you cannot drive home.

Take the time before trial to get your finances in order so that you can pay any possible fines, ASAP fees, and other expenses on time. Most courts will not allow a driver to receive a restricted license until they pay all fines and court costs.

Arrange to take the time off work to go to court or to serve jail time. Also, leave unnecessary valuables (cell phone, cash, watches etc.) at home or with someone else, so you will not risk losing them in the jail's property room if you are sentenced to jail.

If you will need a photo ID less than 60 days after your trial, get a passport. If convicted, the court will confiscate your Virginia license and your temporary restricted license will not include photo ID. You can get a photo ID version of your restricted license from the DMV 30 to 60 days after your trial.

Talk to your attorney about the possibilities of the various sentences, and get your life in order in case of the worst-case scenario.

Can I Get a Continuance?
Continuances are very important and should never be wasted. Continuances can be used to discover what evidence the prosecution has against the driver. The attorney can show up on the day of trial, talk to the police and commonwealth attorney, and find out what evidence they have. Then the attorney can get a continuance in order to prepare a response to that evidence.

Additionally, if the attorney you want to hire is not available on your trial date, your attorney may use a continuance to schedule your court date on a day he is available. However, if you have wasted your continuances you may have to settle for the attorney who is available instead of the attorney who is best.

Also, being granted a continuance may increase the odds that the court will grant the other side a continuance if they ask for one. If the police officer, breathalyzer operator, or other witnesses do not show up at trial, the prosecutor will ask for a continuance and your attorney may ask for the case to be dismissed. However, if the court has already granted you several continuances, the court may be more inclined to grant the Commonwealth a continuance instead of dismissing your case.

Do not put yourself in a position where you will have to waste continuances. Find a quality DUI attorney immediately.

Chapter 12:
"Can I Drive Yet?"

What Happens to Your License after Arrest and
Conviction

Next to going to jail, the worst thing that can happen to
most people is losing their driver's license.
Unfortunately, Virginia is extraordinarily strict about
taking away peoples' right to drive.

There are three types of license suspension that can affect
a person charged with DUI in Virginia: 1) an
administrative suspension – an automatic suspension
where the arresting officer confiscates your license at the
jail; 2) a judicial suspension – a suspension where the
judge suspends your license, and the bailiff confiscates
your license; and 3) a DMV suspension – a suspension
where the DMV sends you a letter after the trial notifying
you that you no longer have the right to drive.

What Is an Administrative Suspension and Which Crimes Apply?

An "administrative suspension" (found in Va. Code §
46.2-391.2) occurs when a driver's license is taken away
after an arrest for DUI or Refusal to Submit to a Breath
Test. Administrative suspensions apply *only* to drivers
who are charged with refusal to submit to a breath/blood
test, or who are charged with DUI based on a BAC of .08
or more (unless they are under 21, in which case it is a

BAC of .02 or more). There should be no administrative suspension for DUI if you blew below .08.

If you have a Virginia driver's license, the officer will confiscate it at the scene or at the station and will make you sign a notification of administrative suspension. If you have an out-of-state license the police should not confiscate your physical license but instead will make you sign a piece of paper that notifies you that you are banned from driving in Virginia for a certain period of time.

If the police confiscated your out-of-state license or if the police lost your license, you should contact an attorney immediately to aid you in getting your license back.

The Administrative Suspension Period
Administrative suspensions last only seven days for first time offenders, but drivers with prior DUI or refusal to submit convictions will be suspended for 60 days or until the day of trial (whichever comes first). Drivers charged with DUI third may be administratively suspended until their trial.

Drivers can appeal an administrative suspension and/or receive a restricted driver's license before trial. However, drivers should make sure that any attorney contract they sign includes help with the administrative suspension process.

What Happens to My Actual License When the Police Take It?

When a driver's license is confiscated, the police turn it in to the magistrate with a copy of the notice of administrative suspension. The magistrate will then give your license to the court clerk. The court clerk holds onto the license until the suspension period is over, and then mails it back to the driver at the address on their license.

Consequently, the driver will not get the license back until the administrative suspension is up and the license goes through the mail. If the driver's address is wrong on the driver's license, then the driver may not receive their license. Drivers may request that the court clerk hold the license for pick-up at the court clerk's office.

If the post office, clerk, magistrate, or officer loses your license you can report your license lost to the DMV and get it back after your administrative suspension period has expired.

If your license was issued by another state, the police are not supposed to confiscate your license and the administrative suspension only applies to driving in Virginia. This means that if you are arrested for DUI in Virginia and you have an out-of-state driver's license, you can drive anywhere *except* Virginia during the suspension period. Virginia driver's license holders, however, cannot drive anywhere during the suspension period, even if they are outside of Virginia.

Appealing an Administrative Suspension

A driver can appeal an administrative suspension. If a driver appeals the suspension, the court must let the driver appear before a judge within the next business day. Contact an attorney immediately to see whether you may be able to void the administrative suspension. Also, read your attorney-client contract carefully to determine whether you will be charged extra for an administrative suspension appeal.

Judicial Suspension

The second way that Virginia may revoke your right to drive is through the judicial process. If a person is found guilty of his first DUI, the judge (by law) must suspend his license for 12 months. A second offense in ten years requires a mandatory suspension of three years. A third or fourth offense will result in an indefinite suspension of the right to drive.

Conviction of refusal to submit to a breath/blood test with no prior convictions will result in a 12-month suspension of your driver's license, and the suspension will be in addition to whatever license suspensions you may have pending for DUI or other charges.

For all types of DUI and refusal to submit, the judicial license suspension is mandatory and neither the judge nor the prosecutor has the power to convict a person without also suspending their license for the full time period. If the court forgets to suspend the license for the full period, the Virginia DMV will administratively suspend the license.

The court may, under certain circumstances, grant a driver a restricted driver's license. Restricted driver's licenses are by definition "restrictive." A restricted driver's license limits the times and places you can drive, and these restrictions must be strictly obeyed. If they are not, the driver may be charged with additional criminal charges and violate their probation.

A first-time DUI offender may be granted a restricted license immediately or upon registering for ASAP, but a second conviction for DUI in ten years means no restricted license will be granted for four months. If the second conviction is within five years, the driver must wait one year to apply for a restricted license. A third-time offender must wait three years to apply for a restricted license.

CDL holders cannot be given restricted licenses, and some out-of-state driver's will not be given a restricted license. Drivers convicted of refusal to submit are *not* able to receive a restricted license during the duration of their suspension for refusal to submit.

A driver's first conviction for refusal requires a 12-month suspension without a restricted license. If a driver has been convicted of refusal or DUI in the past ten years, then conviction for refusal will mean three years without any driving. A third conviction comes with a mandatory indefinite suspension.

DMV Suspension

The final way that a driver can lose his license from a DUI conviction is if the DMV takes away their license. The Virginia DMV will suspend or revoke a Virginia license because of excessive demerit points or for administrative reasons.

Almost all of the DUI and DUI-related offenses (including refusal) are six-point offenses. The DMV has complete control over the demerit point system and there is nothing that a judge can do to alter the number of points assigned.

If a driver loses their right to drive because of excessive demerit points while on a restricted license, the Virginia DMV will take away their restricted license.

For minor drivers, any demerit point conviction means they must attend a driver improvement class. Failure to do so within 90 days results in a license suspension until the program is completed. A second point conviction results in a 90-day license suspension. A third will result in a suspension for one year or until the offender reaches age 18, whichever is longer.

For adults, the accumulation of eight demerit points in 12 months or 12 points in 24 months results in an advisory letter from the DMV. The accumulation of 12 demerit points within 12 months or 18 points in 24 months results in a mandatory driver improvement class and six months of DMV driving probation followed by 18 months on a control period. The driver improvement program must be

139

completed within 90 days or the driver's license will be suspended indefinitely.

Consequences of Demerit Points in Virginia (Adult Drivers)		
	within 12 months	within 24 months
8 points	Letter from DMV	Nothing
12 points	Mandatory driver-improvement class	Letter from DMV
18 points	Mandatory 90-day license suspension + driver-improvement class + probation for six months	Mandatory driver-improvement class
24 points	Mandatory 90-day license suspension + driver-improvement class + probation for six months	Mandatory 90-day license suspension + driver-improvement class + probation for six months

The accumulation of 18 points in 12 months or 24 points in 24 months results in a mandatory 90-day license suspension. Once that period has expired, offenders must complete driver improvement classes before their license can be restored. After restoration, they will be on probation for six months and a control period for 18 months.

If drivers are convicted of any traffic offense while on DMV probation, their licenses will be suspended. Their licenses will be suspended for 45 days for a three-point violation, 60 days for a four-point violation, and 90 days for a six-point violation. Once they finish the suspension period, they will be placed on probation for an additional 6 months followed an 18 month control period.

If a driver gets any demerit point moving violation while on a control period, the DMV will place that driver back on probation for another 6 months, followed by another 18 months of control period.

A driver should *always* get a copy of his driving record before trial, so he can determine whether he is in danger of a DMV suspension. A DMV suspension can jeopardize a driver's restricted license.

The DMV can also administratively suspend a Virginia driver's license. This can happen when the DMV believes a person is no longer physically or mentally able to drive safely. In DUI cases, this typically occurs after an accident by an elderly or disabled driver. In those cases, the DMV sends a letter to the driver requiring them to be evaluated by several doctors within a specific time period in order to avoid suspension.

The DMV may also administratively suspend a license when a driver gets an out-of-state DUI or refusal conviction. Because out-of-state courts cannot suspend a Virginia license, if a Virginia driver receives a DUI or refusal conviction in another state, Virginia may suspend the driver's license on behalf of the foreign state.

Many other states have a similar policy regarding DUI convictions in Virginia. If you have an out-of-state driver's license consult your local DMV or a local traffic attorney to find out your state's policy regarding Virginia DUI or refusal convictions.

The Virginia DMV will also administratively suspend a Virginia license if a Virginia court convicts a driver of DUI or refusal but the court forgets to suspend the license or improperly grants a restricted license.

Restrictive Driver's License
Not everyone can get a restricted license. Some out-of-state drivers and all Commercial Driver's License holders will not be issued a restricted license. Drivers convicted of refusal cannot get a restricted license. Drivers with shifting work schedules or work locations may not be able to get a license that fits their needs. And even if the law allows a restricted license, a judge may choose not to grant one.

However, if the judge does grant a restricted license, that judge will have some discretion as to how, when, and where you get to drive.

A restrictive driver's license allows limited driving for work as well as to and from school, child care, medical treatment, ASAP, court-ordered child visitation, religious worship, probation visits, and delayed turn-in at the jail.

Some driving activities listed on the restricted license require the applicant to include the location name and its address. The judge will also approve the exact times you are allowed to drive (e.g "drive from home to work at 7:15am-8:00am Mon-Fri, drive from work to home at 5:00pm-5:45pm Mon-Fri"). Amending a restricted license requires appearing before a judge in most courts.

Other activities' locations and times are not stated on the restricted license but instead require the driver to carry written proof whenever they drive. For instance, if you drive for work, your employer must provide you with a written notice of where you are driving to and what time you will be driving.

Driving outside those times or driving anywhere but an approved location will result in a conviction for driving on a suspended license and a probation violation. Driving to the grocery store or stopping to get food at a drive-through is not allowed.

A judge may require a driver to register for ASAP or get a favorable evaluation from ASAP before they are allowed to receive a restricted license. Most courts require drivers to pay all their fines and court costs before they will issue a restricted license.

In some courts (especially Circuit Court) a driver applies for the restricted license at trial, but the license is not issued until days or weeks later. Talk to your attorney about this possibility so you do not get stranded without a license.

The trial court judge or the court clerk's office will set the terms and conditions (if any) on when and how you can get a restricted driver's license. Make sure your attorney-client contract includes helping you apply for a restricted license and also registering for ASAP.

Ignition Interlock

Ignition interlock is a system that is given as a condition for receiving a restricted driver's license. Starting in July 1st, 2012, ignition interlock became mandatory anytime a driver is convicted of any form of DUI.

The interlock system is a portable breathalyzer that is installed in cars driven or owned by the defendant. The system comes with a key-chain breathalyzer, and the driver must blow into the breathalyzer to start the car. He then must blow again every 15-30 minutes to keep the car running.

If the device detects a BAC of .02 or above, the car will not start or will shut off. Furthermore, the results of the test are saved electronically and sent to ASAP. A driver who blows a .02 or more may be charged with a probation violation, and the driver may have to serve the remainder of the suspended jail time, pay the remainder of the suspended fine, and may lose their restricted license.

The ignition interlock system may cost approximately $70-$110 to install, and $60 a month (per system) to lease and maintain. The driver will need one system for each car he owns or drives (except when driving a company vehicle in some situations). A driver can sometimes petition the court to remove ignition interlock after six months has passed. Talk to your attorney about this possibility.

Operating a vehicle without ignition interlock after being required to do so by the court is a crime, and blowing into someone else's ignition interlock is also a serious crime. The DMV will not reinstate a driver's license until they have installed ignition for at least six months regardless of whether that driver owns a car or gets a restricted license.

Reinstating Your License
A driver who was found guilty of DUI cannot get his driving privileges back until he pays all his fines and court costs, his suspension period has expired, he has paid approximately $175 in DMV reinstatement fees, *and* he has been reissued a driver's license from the DMV.

If a driver has any concerns about whether (or how) he can get his license back, he should contact the DMV and request a "compliance summary". The summary will spell out all conditions necessary for the driver to get his license back.

Out-of -State Driver's License

The Virginia government (police, judge, or DMV) can suspend an out-of-state license holder's right to drive in Virginia, but they are not allowed to confiscate an out-of-state license. If the police or bailiff confiscates your out-of-state driver's license, you should notify your attorney immediately to begin the process of getting it back. Once again, check your attorney-client contract to make sure your attorney will not charge you extra for these services.

If you have an out-of-state license, you can still drive anywhere *outside* of Virginia unless your own state suspends your license. Each state has unique rules and processes for determining whether to suspend a license based on a Virginia DUI conviction.

Out-of-state drivers will required to pay a license reinstatement fee at the Virginia DMV before their privilege to drive in Virginia will be restored. Out-of-state driver's should request a Virginia DMV compliance summary if they have any questions about whether their privilege to drive in Virginia has been restored.

What Happens if I Drive While My License Is Suspended?

Driving after your license is suspended for DUI is a Class 1 misdemeanor. It can lead to up to 12 months of jail time, one year of additional license suspension, 120 days of vehicle impound, and it can cost thousands in fines, fees, and costs. Driving on a revoked or suspended license will typically violate the terms of your probation and result in substantial additional jail time.

Many people think that they can get away with a little bit of driving while their license is suspended. However, an officer in a cruiser can pull up behind you in traffic, run your license plate in seconds, and potentially tell whether you are suspended. Driving on a suspended license is one of the most common criminal charges in Virginia.

Chapter 13:
"What is Going to Happen at Trial?"
What to Expect on the Day of Trial

The typical judicial experience in Virginia varies wildly between jurisdictions. In Hampton, some judges moves so fast that drivers plead and are sentenced before they reach the front of the courtroom.

In other jurisdictions, the court moves very slowly. In Rockbridge County, a single courtroom may have less than 20 cases a day, while a single Fairfax County courtroom may have up to 200 cases before noon.

Each jurisdiction also has its own method of running the courts. Most courts begin the docket by getting the quick business out of the way: motions, continuances, and unrepresented drivers pleading guilty. Larger courts often organize the cases by police officer, starting with the officers with the fewest cases.

Usually, the courts will call out the names of people without attorneys, setting aside the defense attorneys' cases for last. It is always important to sit in the courtroom and listen for your name unless your attorney counsels you otherwise.

Negotiating Before the Trial
When the court begins the docket, the commonwealth attorneys will often use this time to talk to police officers, witnesses, and defense attorneys. Within the first 45

minutes or so, the defense attorney will often have an opportunity to hear the evidence against the driver and start negotiations for a possible plea deal.

Smaller jurisdictions may allow the defense attorney to see the evidence or negotiate the plea before the trial date, but in larger jurisdictions, the prosecutors may refuse to negotiate until the day of the trial because they are too busy or unable to review the case before the day of the trial.

What If I Am Late to Trial?
Make sure you know the exact time, date, and location of your case. Show up early. Failure to show up at trial may result in the judge issuing a bench warrant for your arrest. You may lose your bail and be forced to wait in jail until your new trial date. You do not want to have this happen to you, so plan to arrive early and allow time for flat tires, traffic, or choked security lines.

If you know you are going to be late, notify your attorney as soon as possible. Your attorney may be able to delay the trial or get a continuance.

Plea Agreements
After a defense attorney has had an opportunity to negotiate with the prosecution, the client will have an opportunity to accept, reject or give a counter offer to the terms of a plea. If the client accepts the terms of the plea, the defense attorney will present the plea agreement to the judge.

Plea agreements are *not* set in stone. After a guilty plea, a judge has the right to alter plea deals if the judge wants to. Most plea agreements are just suggestions to the judge rather than binding agreements. If a judge does alter the agreement, the defense attorney may ask to retract the guilty plea. If the judge does not retract the guilty plea, the defense attorney may appeal to the Circuit Court and retry the case. However, most judges rarely alter plea agreements.

Most prosecutors will not and cannot make any promises regarding restricted licenses. At best, the prosecution will agree not to contest your application for a restricted license. Consequently, getting a restricted license and the conditions within a restricted license are left up to the judge. It is essential to have an experience DUI attorney who can predict your specific judge's likely response to a restricted license application.

Trial
If a client does not accept a plea agreement, he can still decide whether to plead guilty, not guilty, or no-contest (there is no significant difference between pleading "guilty" and "no-contest"). The defendants pleading "not guilty" are usually the last people in the courtroom to be heard.

If a client pleads "guilty" or "no-contest," the court will usually only discuss the issue of what the sentence should be. If the client pleads "not guilty," the court will have a trial and discuss the issue of guilt. If the defendant is found guilty, the court will then discuss the sentence and the restricted license if applicable.

Paying Fines and Costs
After the judge rules, a client who is found not guilty is free to go. If a client is found guilty, he will have to pay fines, fees, and court costs. He must also register for ASAP within 15 days of the trial or his release from jail.

Most courts will allow a driver to set up a payment plan for a small additional price. Most courts will allow the driver to postpone payment if arranged with the court in advance. A few courts have community service programs that they offer in exchange for paying fines or costs. Most drivers will never hear about any of these options unless they have an attorney who has agreed to represent them through the post-conviction process.

If a driver does not pay his court costs or comply with the ASAP program, he may be found in violation of the terms of his probation and sent to jail. Failing to pay fines and register for ASAP may also prevent the driver from getting a restricted driver's license. A driver cannot get his license back after the 12-month period without paying all the fines and costs and successfully completing ASAP.

What Do I Do if I Am Late or Miss My Trial Date?
If you are going to be late or miss your trial date, call your attorney immediately. If you can contact your attorney *before* the judge issues a bench warrant, the attorney can ask the judge to either push the client's case

to the very end of the docket or ask for a continuance and set a new trial date.

If the client does not talk to his attorney until *after* a bench warrant is issued, the attorney can file a motion to appear before a judge and ask the judge to remove the bench warrant. The client must appear before the judge with his attorney. If the judge refuses to remove the warrant, the judge will set bail and the client will be arrested or issued a summons for the charge of failure to appear.

What Happens if the Officer Does Not Show?
If the officer or any other witness does not show up to the trial, the prosecution can choose to ask for a continuance, drop the charges or attempt to move forward without their witness. If the prosecution asks for a continuance, the judge will listen to the opinions of the prosecution and defense attorney and decide whether to continue the case. If the defense has received continuances in the past or if it is the case's first court date the odds of the prosecution receiving a continuance may be higher.

If the witness does not have a good excuse for being absent, the judge may force the prosecution to move forward with the case. At that point the prosecution can either drop the charges or attempt to try the case without the witness.

If the prosecution drops the charges then the prosecution has the option of bringing back the charges later. If it is a misdemeanor then the charges cannot be brought back later than one year after the offense date. If the charge is a felony then the prosecution may bring it back anytime. If your charges are dropped by the prosecution your attorney can advise you on the likelihood of the charges being brought back.

If there is a trial and the judge dismisses the charges, those charges cannot be brought back by the prosecution.

Getting a Restricted License
A driver found guilty of DUI (but not refusal to submit) may be granted the right to receive a restricted license by the judge. The judge may require the driver to pay fines and costs, or get evaluated by ASAP prior to being granted a restricted license.

To apply for a restricted license, the driver will need to supply the court with the exact times and locations of some of the places to which they need to drive (such as work, school, and church). If the driver wants to drive to health care providers, school, or day care, they must have documentation containing the times and locations while driving.

The judge may or may not grant the restricted license, or the judge may grant it under the conditions of the court's choosing. This can be problematic for clients who go to work at different times or locations each day. The more complicated your work schedule the less likely it is that a judge will give you a restricted license. It is essential to have an attorney available to help with the application process.

If a driver is not happy with their restricted license or if they need to change their restricted license, they may make a motion to amend their license. Also, a driver may petition the court for removal of the ignition interlock system after 6 months if they have had no further alcohol-related violations of the interlock requirements.

Make sure your attorney-client contract guarantees your attorney's help getting a restricted license.

Once a driver gets his restricted license, he must carry it with him whenever he drives. Furthermore, he may only drive during the times stated on the license and between the locations approved on the license.

The restricted license issued by the court on a green 8.5" x 11" piece of paper is a temporary restricted license. The driver has only 60 days to go to the DMV and get a permanent restricted license before the court's temporary restricted license expires.

As a condition of a restricted license: 1) the drive must have their first ASAP meeting within 15 days of trial or release from jail, and 2) the ignition interlock system must be installed and the drive must give ASAP proof of installation within 30 days of the trial. The driver must pay for the systems installation and monthly maintenance.

If a judge grants a driver the right to drive for their employment the driver does not need to have interlock installed on company vehicles unless they are an owner or part owner of the company.

If a driver has a commercial driver's license (CDL), the DMV will not issue a restricted license even if the judge approves it. If you have a CDL, make sure that you inform your attorney as soon as possible.

Suspended Sentences
Typically, a judge will hand down a sentence with the majority of the jail time and fines suspended. This kind of sentence is a form of "inactive probation." This means that the driver is on probation but does not have to report to a probation officer. Instead, the driver must complete the ASAP program, pay fines and costs, and avoid any other convictions or serious traffic offenses.

The judge will also declare a period of time for the probation to end. Typically, this period is one year. If the driver violates the conditions of probation (e.g. does not comply with ASAP or gets another criminal conviction), he may be required to appear before the judge to determine how much of the suspended sentence he will have to serve. Many judges typically require the entire suspended sentence be served for any violation of probation. The suspended jail time will be in addition to the sentence for any subsequent convictions.

If you have any suspended sentences or probation from a previous conviction tell your attorney. Also, make sure you hire a DUI attorney who will walk you through the ASAP and restrict driver's license registration process, so you can avoid accidentally failing to comply with your probation.

Registering for ASAP
A driver who is required to attend the Alcohol Safety Action Program ("ASAP") as part of his probation, must register 15 days after the trial or upon release from jail. Without registering for ASAP, the driver cannot get a restricted driver's license and may even be sent to jail for violating their probation.

As part of registration, drivers will have an intake interview and be assigned a case manager who will decide whether they have a "substance abuse problem." Drivers without any special substance abuse issues will typically be assigned to a 20-hour, 10-week program that meets once a week at the same time every week for two hours a session.

ASAP can also force drivers to undergo drug testing and will typically require 100% abstinence from drugs and alcohol. Failure to live up to ASAP's requirements can result in a probation violation and prevent a driver from getting his license back.

Those drivers with alcohol or other substance abuse problems will enter more rigorous programs depending on their specific addictions and program availability. The more intensive programs can cost thousands of dollars and involve anything up to mandatory inpatient rehabilitation.

Driver's with elevated BACs, multiple DUI convictions, drug convictions or who have substance abuse issues are more likely to be ordered into the more expensive and more rigorous treatment programs.

Failure to sign up for or complete ASAP can cause a driver to violate his probation. A driver will not be taken off probation or given back their license if they do not fully comply with ASAP.

When Can I Drive Again?
A Virginia driver who was found guilty of DUI must surrender his license to the bailiff of the court. If a driver does not turn over their license to the court, the suspension will still take effect but the suspension period will not begin until the physical license has been surrendered. This means that if a Virginia driver has a 12-month suspension period, they will get their license back 12 months after they surrender not 12 months after the trial. Always surrender you Virginia license immediately to avoid an extended suspension period.

Drivers do not get their license back automatically after the end of the suspension period. A driver who has completed the suspension period cannot get his driver's license back until they have paid the DMV reinstatement fee and have been issued a driver's license from the DMV.

If a driver has any concerns about whether they can get their license back, the driver should contact the Virginia DMV and request a "compliance summary." The summary will spell out all conditions necessary for the driver to have their driving privileges restored.

Expungements

In Virginia, a driver's criminal record is public information and can be accessed online through the Virginia Supreme Court's website.

This same information is also sent to a law enforcement data base in Richmond and then gathered by various other databases. This information is made available to the public through numerous private investigations and background search companies. Each person's criminal record contains a record of his arrests and convictions.

In Virginia, convictions cannot be expunged. A driver may have the record of his arrest removed from public records only if the charges were dismissed, nolle prosequi (dropped), or the driver is found "not guilty." The record of the defendant's arrest will be sealed the same way that juvenile records are sealed.

If a driver wants to have his record expunged, he should contact a DUI attorney after the charges have been finalized.

Chapter 14:
"Should I Appeal?"
Pros and Cons of Appealing a Conviction

When a person is arrested for a misdemeanor in Virginia, he is tried in the General District Court (GDC) of the county, city, or town where the crime was committed. A conviction in GDC can be appealed to the Circuit Court of Virginia within ten calendar days.

An appeal to the Circuit Court, is an appeal by right, meaning that the defendant only has to ask for the appeal to get it. No one can deny the defendant the request for an appeal to Circuit Court as long as it is filed properly within ten days.

If the defendant appeals to the Circuit Court, several things will happen. The GDC judge may issue an appeal bond if the defendant was sentenced to jail, and the GDC's sentence and conviction will be erased. This means that the driver's license will be returned and the driver will be released from custody once an appeal bond is paid.

Make sure you make arrangements for your attorney to help you with your appeal prior to your trial in General District Court. If you have already retained your attorney for your appeal and you are sentenced to jail in General District Court, your attorney can usually prevent you from ever being physically placed in jail.

If you have not made such arrangements, then you may have to arrange to retain your attorney or file your own appeal while sitting in jail. This may lead to you spending unnecessary time behind bars.

Your new trial will be held in the Circuit Court. The Circuit Court will conduct a completely new trial. The Circuit Court judges are not bound by any decision made by the General District Court judge. A Circuit Court judge can punish a driver more leniently, more severely, or not at all. This is called a trial *de novo*.

The Circuit Court is a different court system than the General District Court. The Circuit Court has different procedural rules. For example, you can get a jury trial in Circuit Court, but you cannot have a jury in General District Court.

The Circuit Court in some jurisdictions is located in different buildings or even different cities than the General District Court, so make sure you know where you are supposed to go on the day of your appeal.

There are additional court costs associated with Circuit Court. For a misdemeanor DUI case the additional court cost is about $150. If a driver wants a jury, that will be an additional $400 per trial day. Circuit Court can also have different requirements for getting a restricted operator's license so talk to your attorney before appealing.

The decisions of the Circuit Court can be appealed to the Virginia Court of Appeals and then to the Supreme Court of Virginia. However, these courts can choose whether or not to hear those appeals. The Court of Appeals and Virginia Supreme Court will only reverse decisions by the Circuit Court if the Circuit Court made a serious mistake.

Felony DUI cases follow a different path. Felony DUI cases typically involve a preliminary hearing in GDC to determine only if there is enough evidence to justify a trial. After that, the felonies are tried in the Circuit Court.

As always, a driver should read their attorney-client contract carefully. Some attorneys charge additional fees for appeals. Some charge extra if a felony DUI goes beyond the preliminary hearing. Others charge extra if there is a jury trial. Make sure you discuss the prices of these various appeals and processes with your attorney so that you can prepare financially.